History of India from Earliest Times Upto 300 CE

About the Author

Jayanta Baidya is a Historian and Assistant Professor of Indian History. Jayanta Baidya started his teaching career as a lecturer at a Bangabasi College. Since 2003, he spent seven years as a Assistant Professor of History at the Asansol Girls' College. He got his M.Phil. for his thesis "Kautilya's Arthasastra: Assessment of Morality". In 2010 he became Assistant Professor of history in newly established Shirakole Mahavidyalaya. Mr. Baidya did his graduation in History from Jadavpur University, Kolkata. As a keen observer of Ancient India, he completed his M.A. in History from Jadavpur University. He has been engaged in research on Ancient India for a decade. He is a life member of several academic bodies and writes on The Caste System, Rigvedic India, The Aryans, Jainism, Buddhism, Ancient Indian Polity, The Harappan Culture, Pre-Historic Races and Cultures in India, Social Religious, Economic and Cultural Conditions in Post-Mauryan Times (181 B.C.-320 A.D.) etc.

History of India from Earliest Times Upto 300 CE

Jayanta Baidya

CONCEPT PUBLISHING COMPANY PVT. LTD.
NEW DELHI-110059

ISBN: 978-93-5439-032-6 (HB)

ISBN: 978-93-5439-035-7 (PB)

First Published 2022

Published and Printed by

Concept
Since 1974

Concept Publishing Company Pvt. Ltd.
A/15-16, Commercial Block, Mohan Garden
New Delhi-110059 (India)
T : 91 11 41101460, 91 11 25351460, 91 11 25351794
E : publishing@conceptpub.com; *W* : www.conceptpub.com

Cataloging in Publication Data--Courtesy: D.K. Agencies (P) Ltd. <docinfo@dkagencies.com>

Baidya, Jayanta, author.
History of India from earliest times upto 300 CE / Jayanta Baidya.
pages cm
Includes bibliographical references.
ISBN 9789354390326 (HB)
ISBN 9789354390357 (PB)

1. India--History--To 324 B.C. 2. India--History--324 B.C.-1000 A.D. I. Title.

LCC DS425.B35 2022 | DDC 934 23

PREFACE

Reading makes a man perfect,
Meetings-conferences make a man just and
Writing makes a man a proper human being.
— Francis Bacon

I have tried to write the book 'History of Ancient India' for the benefit of the students. The book is written in simple language. As Thomas Carlyle put it, "the appreciation of the books is the true knowledge of the world today." So any book should be read. In that sense no book can be bad or evil. This belief is etched in my mind by my sister Sima Baidya, a professor in the Department of International Relations at Jawaharlal Nehru University in New Delhi. I am grateful to Manas Dey of Concept Publications for entrusting me to write this book, 'History of Ancient India'. I am indebted deeply to Ashok Mittal of Concept Publications Pvt. Ltd. for his constant help, support and guidance. Many professors and students from West Bengal, Tripura, and Bangladesh have given me their valuable suggestions and opinions at different times. Their feedback has inspired and educated me a lot. I am forever indebted to them. Nevertheless, I am the person who is solely responsible for spelling errors and other mistakes. I hope everyone will look at it with an apologetic and kind heart. I would heartily welcome any reader's opinion for the betterment of this book. I would consider this book of mine a fruitful one if it is of little use to them for whom it is written with great passion and honesty. In the end I would like to mention that this book would not have been written without the support of my wife Mrs. Sanjita Baidya and mother Mrs. Rekha Baidya.

CONTENTS

HISTORICAL ELEMENTS OF ANCIENT INDIA

1

G.P. Singh mentions Rig Veda, Sama Veda, Epic poetries, Puranas, Buddhist and Jain literatures as Historical Elements of Ancient India. From these resources, we can have a clear picture of social, political and financial life of that epoch. Shailendranath Sen upholds one argument in his book 'Ancient Indian History and Civilization' stating that one of the major problems of Historical Elements of Ancient India is the lack of sequentially and consistently written history. We did not have historians like Herodotus, Thucydides, Livy, Tacitus or Polybius during that period. So, archaeological evidences were important as we did not have any written documentation of the period. That is why Al-Beruni too commented that "Though Hindus have excelled in philosophy, literature, science and religion, still they are very indifferent towards the history of their livelihood". History is nothing but truthful facts of the past. We could not have gathered detailed factual descriptions of Ancient India if we follow a particular time period of ancient India. According to Ranabir Chakravarti "elements and evidences of Ancient India is incomplete, fragmentary and scattered". For these reasons much emphasis is stressed upon the archaeological evidences to gather knowledge of ancient India. We are accused of a lack of historical sense when we attempt to write the history of Ancient India. Proper history of India had not been documented either because of the lack of historical sense or indifference of Indian sentiment towards mortal life. Ramesh Chandra Majumdar believes that "Indians did not have a lack of sense of history or historical elements, what they actually lack is their keenness and desire to write a true account of history of literary quality". Thus, there are two types of historical elements available while writing the history of ancient India: (i) Literary Material, and (ii) Archaeological Material.

Literary Material

Upinder Singh and Nayanjot Lahiri consider literary material as evidence of Ancient India in their book "Ancient India: New Research". The literary materials of Ancient India are generally divided into two categories:

(i) Indigenous Literary Material, and
(ii) Foreign Literary Material. The indigenous literary materials are further divided into two categories:
  (i) Religious literature, and
  (ii) Secular literature.

Religious Literature

Swami Satyaprakash Saraswati comments that the theism of Vedas is nothing but a simple, straightforward and unadulterated monotheism. As the presence of the soul is acknowledged through the limb movement of the body, likewise Almighty Lord could be realized if we attentively watch the well-designed mobility of the Creator God. The major portion of the Ancient Indian literature is religious literature. The religious literature is further divided into five sub-categories—

(i) Vedic Literature,
(ii) Theology,
(iii) Buddhist-Jain Literature,
(iv) Epic Poetry, and
(v) Puranas.

Vedic Literature

Pandit Satyakam Vidyalankar mentions some important aphorisms of the Vedas in his book "The Holy Vedas" where religious issues are combined with social and ethical issues. *Rig Veda* states "Come! Be

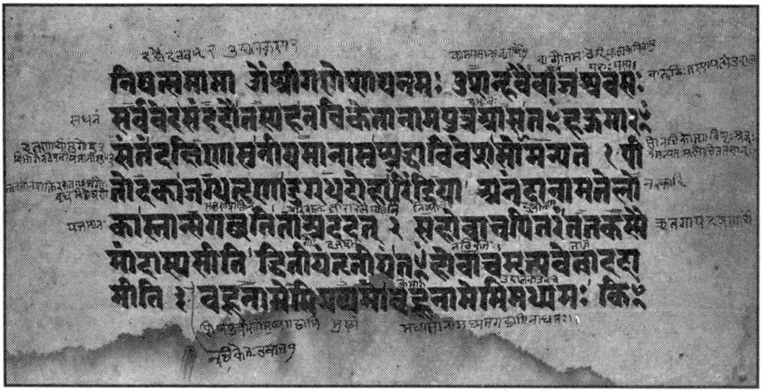

A manuscript page showing verses 1.1.1 to 1.1.3 of the Katha Upanishad

the servant of the Lord. Give something to the poor and needy". *Sama Veda* says, "The truly righteous and pious men are always sweet-spoken and compassionate towards others". According to *Yajur Veda* "Don't say anything in a hoarse voice. Bitter words must not come out of mouth". *Atharva Veda* mentions "O mankind! Work together for the welfare of the people". There are four Vedas –

(i) Rig Veda: This Veda consists of compilation of mantras uttered at the Yajna ceremony of the Aryan along with war annals of ten kings and livelihood of Aryans.
(ii) Sama Veda: A compilation of number of verses of Rig Veda.
(iii) Yajur Veda: Approved code of conduct for the priests who perform Yajna.
(iv) Atharva Veda: It is composed of incantations and miracles. Though these four Vedas are religious literatures, still one can gather information on the socio-political and fiscal issues of the Aryan period. The appendix of Veda is Brahmana and the appendix of Brahmana is Aranyaka and Upanishad.

Shastra or Smriti

Even after being Hindus, still we have dispute with each other on Shastras. One group says that these things are written in these Shastras. Other group contests this argument by quoting from different Shastras. So the dispute remains about which religious scripture to follow and which not to. However, from these theologies we come to know about the contemporary society, economy, and political scenario so on and so forth. The social and family issues are discussed in "Manusmriti" and "Yajnavalkya Smriti". Marriage custom, the position of women, family event, social norms, restrictions and advice of that epoch are described in the theologies. In those religious scriptures or Shastras (except Vedas) where life is remembered and explained are known as 'Smriti Shastra'. Among these 'Smriti Shastra'-s, we have

(i) 'Manusmriti'
(ii) 'Yajnavalkya Smriti'
(iii) 'Parashar Smriti'
(iv) 'Atri Smriti'
(v) 'Vishnu Smriti'
(vi) 'Katyayana Smriti'
(vii) 'Brihaspati Smriti'
(viii) 'Vyas Smriti' etc.

Buddhist and Jain Literatures

Buddhist and Jain literatures are also an important source of the true portrayal of the social system of Ancient India. The Jain wrote their religious advices in Prakrit language. 'Agama', the Jain theology, was written in half Magadhi. An important landmark of Jain literature is the appendix part ('Parishishta-Parvan') of a book written by Jain scholar Acharya Hemachandra. The religious Jain texts such as "Bhagavati Sutra" and "Kalpa Sutra" written by Bhadrabahu are also considered as important sources from which we could gather a clear picture of urbanization and economic issues apart from religious practices. For Buddhist literature, "Tripitaka" and "Jataka" are considered as notable literary materials of Ancient India. The Buddhist theology 'Tripitaka' is written in Pali language. There are three parts in this holy book:

(i) 'Vinaya Pitaka',
(ii) 'Sutta Pitaka', and

(iii) 'Abhidhamma Pitaka'. 'Tripitaka', the traditional term for Buddhist scripture, is nothing but the philosophy and compilation of Buddhist advices.

'Vinaya Pitaka' is the monastic rules of conduct for Buddhist monks and nuns. 'Sutta Pitaka' contains the advices of Buddha while 'Abhidhamma Pitaka' is a collection of canonical texts where Buddha's teachings are detailed, summarized and analyzed. "Jataka" tales contain story from the previous birth of Gautama Buddha in both human and animal form. So, the contemporary socio-economic conditions could well be derived from these 'Jataka' tales. From "Dipavamsa" and "Mahavamsa", two important Sinhala texts, we can learn many aspects of king Asoka and his next rulers.

Epic Poetry

According to William Buck and Von Nuten, the ancient Sanskrit epic is the "*Ramayana*". According to Hindu belief, the author of this book is Valmiki. This epic describes the ideal of human society as well as the ideal brother, the ideal servant, the ideal wife and the ideal king. In his book "The Ideal of Perfect Life: The Ramayana", K.R. Sundararajan refers fourth century BC as the period of composition of the "*Ramayana*". He thinks that the "*Ramayana*" contains the identity of the patriarchal society of ancient India. In addition, this book provides detailed information about the position of women in the society of that time. According to Dr. Ramesh Chandra Majumdar, the descriptions of the character and civilization of the Indians told in the "*Ramayana*" and the "*Mahabharata*" are not found in any other literature in the world. According to popular belief, Vyasa or Veda Vyasa was the author of the "*Mahabharata*". In *The World History*, Howard Spodeck and Richard Mason report that the volume of the "*Mahabharata*" epic is ten times of the volume of the "Iliad" and the "Odyssey" put together and four times that of the "*Ramayana*". The "*Mahabharata*" is called the 'Fifth Veda' in India. Because this book has given a summary of Hindu religion and Vedic philosophy. As a result, it is wrong to identify the story of the "*Mahabharata*" as merely a myth. It is also said about the "*Mahabharata*" that what is not in the "*Mahabharata*" is nowhere in the whole of India. From these two epics, *"Ramayana"* and *"Mahabharata"*, one can learn about the social customs, caste, nation, society, politics and economy of ancient India.

Puranas

Swami Shivananda commented in his book "The Puranas" that, according to hearsay, the author of the *"Mahabharata"*, Veda Vyasa, compiled the Puranas. Events from creation to destruction have found a place in the Puranas. Apart from this, the genealogy of sages and deities, Hindu cosmology, monarchy, philosophy, etc. have been described in the Puranas. According to Frederick Eden Pargiter, the original Puranas are probably contemporary with the latest written form of the Vedas. Apart from the social and religious life of ancient India, the Puranas also deal with dynasties. The number of Puranas in India is 18. They are:

1. Agni Purana
2. Vayu Purana
3. Bhavishya Purana
4. Mahabhagavat Purana
5. Brahmanda Purana
6. Brahmavavarta Puarana
7. Garuda Purana
8. Vishnu Purana
9. Kurma Purana
10. Linga Purana
11. Markandya Purana
12. Matsya Purana
13. Nareedya Purana
14. Padma Purana
15. Siva Purana
16. Skanda Purana
17. Vamana Purana
18. Varaha Purana.

Secular Literature

Secular literatures are one of the important historical evidences of Ancient India. These literatures are written basically on the livelihood of the people of that era though imagination of the author. Still the societal pictures and issues of Ancient India are evident in those literatures. Contemporary socio-political scenarios are encrypted in "Mrichchhakatika" (The Little Claycart) of Sudraka and "Devichandraguptam" of Vishakhadatta. Kalidasa wrote "Abhijnanasakuntalam", "Raghuvamsa", "Malavikagnimitram" etc. plays during Gupta period. Dandin wrote 'Dashakumaracharita" from which we get a clear picture of social condition of that time. Among the secular literatures, Sangam Literature of Tamilnadu was full of historical evidences of South India. Kallidaikurichi Aiyah Nilkanta Sastri mentions in his book "*A History of South India: From Pre historic Times to the Fall of Vijaynagar*" that the content or the subject matter of Sangam Literature was completely secular. The daily livelihood of the Tamils is portrayed in Sangam Literature. "Silappaatikaram" and "Manimekalai" are two major epic literatures of Tamil written by Prince Ilanko Atikal and Kulavanikan Seethalai Satanar. Two major sub-parts of religious literatures are:

(i) Biography and local anecdotes, and
(ii) Literature on knowledge and science.

Biography and Local Anecdotes

"Harshacharita" is the famous book written by Banabhatta. This book is all about the biography of Indian emperor Harshavardhana. This biographical literature is of high importance as historical evidence. Bilhana wrote another biographical literature 'Vikramankadeva-charita' on the life of Vikramaditya VI, the king of Kalyani Chalukya emperor. The biography of Yashovarman, the king of Kannauj emperor "Gour baho" is written by Vakpati. Sandhyakar Nandi's "Ramacharitam" is written on the narrative of "*Ramayana*" and the Pala king Ramapala. The suppression of 'Kaivarta' rebellion during the reign of Ramapala is also described in this biography.

Kalhana claims that he provides an unbiased history of Kashmir in his famous book "*Rajatarangini*". This book is the earliest source of history that can be labeled as a historical test of this region. This book contains a valuable source of information on the kings of Kashmir.

This Sanskrit book of elegant style also narrates how should a true king be like and how should a king run his government. "Rasmala" written by Someshwara and "Prabandha Kosha" written by Jain scholar Rajashekhara Suri are two important books about the history of 'Gujrat'. Apart from biography and local anecdotes of Ancient Literature, "Arthashastra" written by Kautilya, is considered as an outstanding document of Maurya Empire. In this very book, detailed history of Maurya administration, its politics, economy and social conditions are vividly described. The "Arthashastra" of Kautilya is also praised for providing primary knowledge of Indian military system.

Literature on Knowledge and Science

We have already seen that our country lacked a proper historian and historical accounts of ancient India. But it goes without saying that there was no shortage of books or literature on science in our country during that ancient period. The first thing to mention is the "Charaka Samhita". This book is equally popular with modern physicians. The author of the book is Charaka, the father of Indian medicine. In addition, the medical essay of the surgeon Susruta was equally popular. Amarasimha's book "Amarkosha" was the source of Sanskrit dictionary and knowledge. Aryabhatta was a Gupta-era scientist. The name of the book written by him is "Aryabhatiya". In this book Aryabhatta has explained lunar eclipse, solar eclipse, annual motion, Diurnal motion etc. He also invented the method of calculating decimals. Among his other important works are "Arya-Siddhanta", 'Dashagitikasutra' etc. These were scientific essays. Then we have to mention Varahamihira. He was a famous astronomer. His two most notable books are "Pancha-Siddhantika" and "Brihat-Samhita". Brahmagupta mentioned the gravitational force long before Sir Isaac Newton in his book 'Brahmaphutasiddhant". Scientist Gargi wrote 'Gargi Samhita'. Dhanvantari and Vagbhata wrote medical literature. As a result, there was a great improvement in the writing of science books in ancient India.

Foreign Literary Material

Krishnachandra Sagar in his book 'Foreign Influence of Ancient India' referred to the descriptions of foreign travellers in ancient India. In addition to the influence of foreigners in ancient India, details of the society, economy, politics and culture of the time are found in the accounts of foreign travellers. Foreign literary elements are divided into Greek, Roman, Chinese, etc.

Greek Literary Material

To know the literary material of ancient India, one must mention the literature written by the Greeks. The first book to be mentioned in Greek literature is Herodotus's 'The Histories (The Greek word 'historia' means 'inquiry'). The name 'India' can be known from this book. Herodotus also gives an account of the political situation in north-west India. Then we have to mention the book '*Indica*'. The author of the book is Megasthenes. During the reign of Chandragupta Maurya, he came to India as an envoy of Seleucus. From the book 'Indica' written by Megasthenes, one can know about the seven nations of India at that time. The book 'Indica' was compiled by a Greek traveller named Aryan. Notable among the Greek trevellers were Strabo, Diodorus, Cartius Justin and others. From their writings one can get a great idea of the Indo-Roman trade of that time. The name of the book written by Strabo is "Geographica" (The Geographica or Geography, is an encyclopedia of geographical knowledge, consisting of 17 'books', written in Greek). This book is an invaluable source for learning about the rivers, cities and forests of India at that time. In '*Epitome*', Justin describes the political relationship of Alexander and Seleucus with Chandragupta Maurya. In this text he gave the Greek name of Chandragupta Maurya as Sandrocottus. "*The Periplus of the Erythraean Sea*" was written by an anonymous Greek writer of the time. "*The Periplus of the Erythraean Sea*" is a Roman period guide, anonymously written by a Greek Egyptian in 1st Century BC, to trade and navigation in the Indian Ocean. The description of the Arabian Sea was obtained from the Greek geographer Heraclitus' "On Nature".

Roman Literary Material

Pliny the Elder's book, "Naturalis Historia" or "Natural History", is one of the first to be mentioned in Roman literature. In this book he has given a detailed description of the natural conditions of India. In this book the issue of Indo-Roman trade relations is also vividly discussed. Pliny the Elder's book is written in Latin. Details of geography, history and trade relations of India can be obtained from this book. There are also detailed accounts of Alexander's expedition to India in the book "*Histories of Alexander the Great*" or "Historiae Alexandri Magni" or more fully "Historiarum Alexandri Magni Macedonis Libriqui Supersunt" written by the Roman writer Quintus Curtius Rufus. Another important Roman traveller was Ptolemy. His famous book is called "*Geography*". "*Geography*" (also called the "Geographia") was an informative book on the maritime history of India. The book mentions major places from the Indus to the mouth of the Ganges, including Indian trade.

Elements of Chinese Literature

The material of Chinese literature is equally important to know the history of ancient India. Among the Chinese travellers, Fa-Hien (Faxian) is the first to be mentioned. He came to India during the reign of Chandragupta-II. The name of the book written by him is "A Record of Buddhist Kingdoms (Foguoji)". This book contains a detailed account of the history of the period of Chandragupta-II. The next two most important books one should read in detail to know the history of India are "Han Shu" by Pan Ku or Bangu and "Hou Hanshu" (Book of the Later Han) by Fan-Ye. From these two books one can know the original position of the Kushanas and the description of the arrival of the Kushanas in India. In his book 'Kau-fa-kang-sang-chuen', the Chinese Buddhist scholar I-tsing wrote a biography of Buddhism or the story of Chinese workers traveling to India. The famous Chinese traveller Xuanzang or Hiuen Tsang Xang came to India between 629-645 AD. He came to India during the reign of Harshavardhana. The name of the book written by Hiuen Tsang is "Si-Yu-Ki". Radhakumud Mukherjee wrote about the importance of the books written by the Chinese travellers. The Chinese travellers have come to India to record their beautiful experiences and stories about India.

Archaeological Material

In his book, "Coins of Ancient India form Earliest Times down to the Seventh Century A.D.", Alexander Cunningham mentioned the importance of archaeological material as an element of the history of ancient India. Coin is one of the important elements to know the history of ancient India. However, among the archaeological elements such as:

(a) inscriptions,
(b) coins,
(c) architectural sculptures,
(d) ancient ruins, and
(e) monuments and tombs etc. helped in composing the history of ancient India.

Archaeological evidence of the life, economy, development of rural civilization, urban civilization, transportation system, social conditions of the people of ancient India can be gleaned from it. The period of archaeological material is known with the help of radiocarbon dating method.

Inscription

Vincent Arthur Smith remarked that inscriptions are among the most important archaeological materials in India. These elements are most necessary to know the information of ancient India. The rulers of ancient India used to carve on the walls of hills or caves, on the base of pillars or on copper plates to commemorate their deeds. Royal decrees or king's orders were thus engraved on the walls of hills and caves. What was written by carving is called inscription. The inscriptions are now divided into two parts—local and foreign. Among the native writings, the writings of the Mauryan emperor Asoka are the best. Asoka used Brahmi script in his inscriptions. These inscriptions give a detailed account of the reign of the rulers of ancient India, the land revenue system, administrative matters and religious matters.

Maurya Era: Inscription

One of the major elements of the history of ancient India is the inscription. One of these elements is the inscription of Asoka. This inscription was composed in the Maurya period. Asoka was engraving these inscriptions following the dictatorial rulers of Iran. In 1837, James Prinsep deciphered Asoka's inscription. He was a British Archaeologist and editor of The Asiatic Society. 'Epigraphy' is the science of deciphering scripts or inscriptions. With the help of this knowledge one can know about the relations of Asoka with the neighbouring countries, the borders of Emperor Asoka's kingdom, Asoka's religion and public welfare activities. It is known that the thirteenth inscription of Asoka was changed from 'Bherigosha' or declaration of war to 'Dhammaghosha' or declaration of Dhamma. It is also known from Asoka's inscriptions that Emperor Asoka transformed himself from 'Chandasoka' to 'Dharmasoka'. The inscriptions of Asoka were engraved on (a) boulders, (b) caves, and (c) pillars. It is pertinent to note that Emperor Asoka did not use his name in any of his inscriptions. It is known from the Maski inscription that he used to write 'Devanampiya Piyadasi' instead of his own name. That is, Emperor Asoka was the favourite of the gods. God's beloved. In conclusion, most of Asoka's teachings are written in Prakrit language and Brahmi script. Of the scripts written in the Prakrit language, only Shahbazgarhi and Mansera are written in Kharosthi script for the benefit of the locals. Greek and Aramaic languages and scripts were also used in a few scripts.

Post-Maurya Period: Inscriptions

From 300 to 200 BC, inscriptions of post-Maurya Sunga, Kanva, Saka, Pahlava, Kushan and Satavahana can be identified. These inscriptions were written in Prakrit and Sanskrit. There is a stone wall around the Sanchi mound, where the carved donation papers can be seen.

- (a) Saka Kshatrapa Rudradaman-I in Junagarh inscription,
- (b) Gurjaru-Pratihara ruler Mihira Bhoja (c. 836-885 CE) or Bhoja-I in Gwalior inscription,
- (c) Chalukya King Pulakeshin-II (King c. 610-642 CE) in Aihole inscription,
- (d) Kalinga King Kharavela in Hatigumpha inscription, and
- (e) Deopara Prashasti where the glorious activities of Vijaya Sena of the Sen dynasty is mentioned.

The Deopara Prashasti is a stone inscription (Prashasti) eulogizing the sena kings of Bengal. It was composed by Umapati Dhara. The inscription particularly praises Lakshmana Sena's grandfather Vijaya Sena (c. 1095-1158). Satavahana King Gautamiputra Satakarni's conquests, achievements and social reforms were described in Nasik Prasasti. Nasik Prasasti was engraved by Gautami Balasri, the mother of Gautamiputra Satakarni.

Gupta Age: Inscriptions

Another important inscription of ancient India was the Allahabad Prasasti written by Samudragupta's poet Harisena. This Prasasti was written in Sanskrit. It was written in 33 lines. From the Prasasti of Allahabad one can learn about Samudragupta's Aryavarta, Deccan expeditions and the conquest policy. Two inscriptions are most important to know about the period of Chandragupta II, the son of Samudragupta:

(a) Udayagiri inscription,
(b) Sanchi inscription. Apart from the political issues of the Gupta period, the picture of cultural life is clearly captured in these two inscriptions.

Four more inscriptions from Kumargupta's period have been found. Such as:

(a) Mandasor inscription,
(b) Biharkotta inscription,
(c) Gandhara inscription, and
(d) Tumen inscription. These four inscriptions give an account of the political situation at that time. Among the inscriptions found during Skandagupta's time were:
    (a) Junagarh inscriptions,
    (b) Kanauj inscriptions, and
    (c) Bhitari inscriptions.

Post-Gupta Age: Inscriptions

Two inscriptions were important in learning about the reign of

Shashanka, the ruler of Bengal, a contemporary of Pulakeshin-II and Harshavardhana. The first is the Ganjam Inscription. The second is 'Egra copper-plate'. The Khalimpur copper-plate of the Pala ruler Dharmapala gives an idea of the political situation at that time. A lot of information is available from the inscriptions of Prakash Dharman near Mandasore in Madhya Pradesh and the copper-plate at Jagajjibanpur in Malda district. The Mandasor inscription of Yasodharman was also important. Dr. Bratindnanath Mukherjee, while acknowledging the importance of the copper-plate of Jagajjibanpur, remarked that it was not the first Vigrahapala, but his son Mahendrapala who became the ruler of the Pala Empire as Devapala's successor.

Foreign Inscriptions

Overseas inscriptions are inscriptions found outside India from which much information about India can be obtained. One of the most important inscriptions is the 'Boghaz-Koi' inscription from the Asia Minor region. The arrival of Aryans in India is identified in this inscription. The next important inscription is called Naqsh-e-Rostam. This inscription was engraved in 262 AD. The first Shahpur, the ruler of the Sasanian dynasty in present-day Iran or former Persia, proclaimed the conquest of Hindustan through this inscription. It is further learned that the first Shahpur brought an end to the Kushan Empire in India. The other two inscriptions that mention the name Sindhu or Hindu are—

(a) the 'Hamadan' inscription of King Darius of Persia, and
(b) the Persepolis inscription. Much information about Indo-Persia can be found in the inscriptions 'Persepolis' and 'Naqsh-e-Rostam' by Darius.

According to the Behistun inscription, Punjab and Gandhara were part of the Persian Empire at that time.

Coin of the Persian Era

In his book "The Indian Coins and Currency System", Dineshchanda

Sarkar discusses the importance of currency in the history of ancient India.

(a) With the help of this coin we know the identity of the rulers of ancient India, the boundaries of the kingdom, the year-date and the prosperity of their empire. Coins obtained from tehsils are to be mentioned as examples of ancient coins of India. These date back to around 500 BC. Only from coins do we know about the Bactrian Greeks. The year-dates on the coins give a lot of definite information about the period of the empire of the ancient kings.

(b) Gold coins are often used in ancient India which is indicative of the prosperity of the empire. Similarly, lead or copper coins bear witness to economic decline. The use of gold coins for the prosperity of Rome-India trade can be traced from the Kushan period to the Gupta period.

(c) From the place of receipt of the currency one can know the size of that empire and the identity of trade relations with other regions.

(d) From the pictures of gods and goddesses depicted on the coins, it can be known which religion the king of that time was devoted to.

(e) In addition to idols of gods and goddesses, pictures of ornaments, musical instruments or weapons can be seen on coins.

In the coins of Samudragupta's time, the king is seen playing the harp. From this it is understood that king Samudragupta was fond of music. This science of currency is called 'numismatics'. The coin bears the imprint or patterned design on one side. These coins are called "Punch-marked coins". Gold coins with the name and image of the ruler were found during the reign of Menander, the Greek king of Bahlika country. The first gold coin was introduced in India in the first century during the reign of the Kushan king Vima Kadphises. Kanishka's portrait was found in the Kushan coin. Pashupatinath was depicted in coins during the time of the Kushan kings. From this it is inferred that the Kushan kings were followers of Shaivism. The coin of the first Chandragupta mentions the image of Lakshmi and the coin of the Gupta rulers mentions the word 'Param-Bhagavata'. From this it is inferred that they were Vaishnavas. The coins of the Satavahana kings had pictures of ships. It is understood that maritime trade was going well at that time. In his book "The Coins of Ancient India", S.R. Gayal gave special importance to coins among the archaeological material. For example, the Greek kings ruled in Afghanistan and northern India in the second and first centuries BC are known through the coins. This is the only way to know about some important personalities such as Pantaleon, Agathocles, Euthydemus-II, Antimachos-I, Strato-I, Strato-II, Demetrios-II, Nikator Antiochos-VI Epiphanes, Diomedes, Telephos Euergetes etc.

Architectural-Sculpture

An important section of architectural-sculpture can be seen as an element of the history of ancient India. Relics and evidences of this architecture can be seen in Sarnath, Hastinapur and Taxila. Sculpture was one of the various art forms of Gandhara period. The statue of Gautam Buddha was made by Gandhara artists. Sculptures in Mathura style were found in Sravasti, Kaushambi, Sarnath, Mathura etc. One of the eminent characteristics of Mathura art is the naked idols of Bodhisattvas, Tirthankara, Yaksha idols and Jain Tirthankars. The Vengi and Amravati art was also one of the masterpieces of ancient Indian sculpture. Apart from this, among the other important stupas, the stupas of Sanchi and Amravati are notable. Among the temples of ancient India, the Dashavatara temple at Deogarh, built during the Gupta period, and the brick temple at Bhitargaon in Kanpur were unique. The temple inside Somapura Bihar was remarkably ornate. Architectural and sculptural artifacts were found in South India during the Pallava and Chola periods.The practice of making caves by cutting down hills can be noticed in this Pala period. During the Chola period, during the time of the first Rajaraja-I and Rajendra Chola, a huge Shiva temple was built. It was during this period that the Kumbakonam temple flourished in terms of architecture. According to Sarasikumar Saraswati, the sculptural evidences found in Gandhara, Amravati, Mathura, etc. during the Saka-Kushan period. These evidences took their place in the world of art.

Ancient Ruins

Ancient ruins are a very important element in the history of ancient India. Traces of the oldest civilization in India have been found in these ruins. Notable areas where these ruins are found are Harappa and Mehergarh regions. The antiquity of Indian civilization could be traced back to this ruin. Traces of agriculture were found in the ruins of Kalibangan in Rajasthan. Archaeologists have unearthed the ruins of Harappan cities, revealing the planning and artistic style of those cities. Archaeological remains at Nalanda University have yielded a wealth of information about the university, one of the earliest centres of learning in ancient India. Nobel laureate economist Amartya Sen commented on the university, saying Nalanda University had a true identity across Asia.

Monuments and Tombs

Monuments and tombs are very important elements to know the history of ancient India. Notable among these monuments and tombs are the ancient towns of Sarnath, Taxila, Pataliputra etc. The temples and tombs in present-day Cambodia's Angkor Wat deserve a separate mention. Temples and monuments in the Borobudur region are also one of the tools to know the ancient history. With the help of these ancient relics, evidences, tombs and monuments, it is possible to know the relationship of India with Kambodia and Java. Monuments and tombs reveal the development of ancient Indian civilization, art, architecture and sculpture.

The Importance of Literary and Archaeological Material

The importance of currency in the history of ancient India was mentioned by Alexander Cunningham in his book "Coins of Ancient India from the Earliest Times down to the Seventh Century". This coin is an archaeological element that introduces us to the history of ancient India. The importance of literary material as historical characteristics cannot be denied. In his book "Portraits of a Nation: History of Ancient India", Kamlesh Kapur mentions the importance of historical events in Vedic literature, "*Ramayana*" and "*Mahabharata*" to know the history of ancient India. G.P. Singh underlines the importance of the Puranas. Although this literary element had multiple limitations. (a) The possibility of change in the later period of ancient literature or travelogues cannot be ruled out. The possibility of this change is strong in translating the original literature. (b) Another disadvantage of the literary element is that the stories of the people at the top of the society are usually told here. As a result, the reflection of the whole society is not found in these types of literatures. (c) Most of the literary elements of ancient India were written to praise the rulers and the kings. As a result, finding a neutral history is therefore difficult from there. (d) The literature written in ancient India often mingled with the spiritual and philosophical views of the author. The personal thoughts and religious attitudes of the writers became an obstacle in writing impartial history. (e) Foreign travellers have recorded their travel experience in India. This travelogue was based on folklore and hearsay. As a result, their account of the actual state of the kingdom is not reliable. This is why Ramesh Chandra Majumdar commented in his book "The Vedic Age" that although literary elements have the opportunity to be added later or later, there is no room for such distortions in the case of statements engraved in stone or metal. In his book "Ancient India, History and Archaeology", Dilip Kumar Ganguly remarked that archaeological elements are one of the main elements in knowing the political and cultural history of ancient India. Archaeological material is considered more important than literary material. Because, these elements are much more likely to be neutral. As a result, these archaeological elements are one of the tools to know the social, economic and cultural aspects of that period. Among the archaeological elements to know the history, the archaeological elements of the rulers like Samudragupta, Pulkeshi-II, Gautamiputra Satakarni are the main historical elements. Archaeological material also has limitations. Writer's imaginary qualities were also engraved in archaeological material as the archaeologists were favoured by the king or the regime. Archaeological material in many cases does not mention the year-date. As a result, the description in the inscription was in many cases misleading. Nevertheless, archaeological material is important. Archaeological material can therefore be identified as the 'main anchor in the history of ancient India'.

STONE AGE IN INDIA Detailed Investigation

2

P.T. Srinivasa Ayyangar mentions in his book "The Stone Age in India" that Stone Age lasted for a very long time in India. The period of Stone Age is longer than the historical period. The first part of the Stone Age is called the Old Stone Age or Paleolithic. The Old Stone Age is also called 'Paleolithic Period'. This word is a combination of two Greek words: 'Palaeo' means 'old' and 'Lithos' means 'stone'. Thus, this is how the Ancient Stone Age was named. The period of Old Stone Age started 5,00,000 years ago and ended 10,000 years ago. Approximately from 4,00,000 BC to 2,00,000 BC is referred to as the Old Stone Age. The people of Ancient Stone Age were cavemen. They used to make clothes from animal skin and the tree barks and they used to live by hunting animals. The weapons they made of stone were blunt. They used to live a nomadic life in small groups. Notable regions of the Ancient Stone Age were now-a-days Chennai, Mumbai, Hyderabad, Madhya Pradesh, Rajasthan, Orissa, Sabarmati and Narmada valley, Soanian (Soan) Valley of Punjab (now-a-days Pakistan). The use of fire was not visible in this era. They spent their time searching for food. They did not know how to cook food. Hence, they ate raw foods. They did not eat any cooked food. The people of the period built their homes in caves and on the branches of the trees. They used to go from one place to another in search of food. The evolution of the Ancient Stone Age was seen to have taken place for a long time. The people of this period did not have the knowledge of cultivation or agriculture. Fruits and raw meat were their staple food. They used different types of stoned weapons for hunting animals. According to Hasmukh Dhirajlal Sankalia, the people of the Ancient Stone Age used to live in different

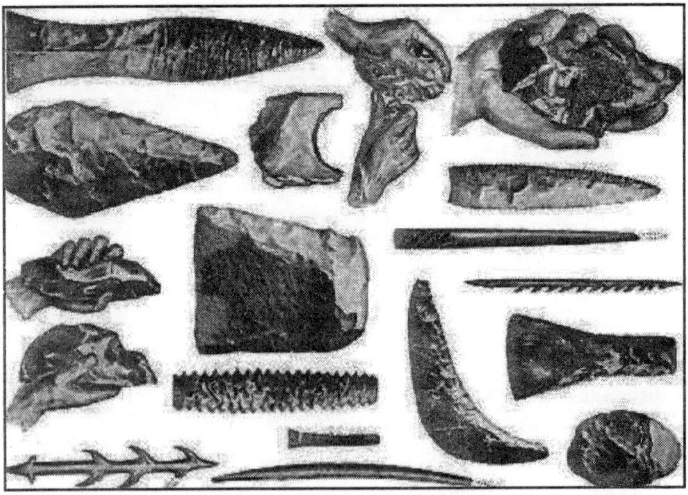

Stone Age Tools and Weapons

parts of India. Hand axe was used in that period. This hand axe was found in the basin of the Soan River. Nicholas Patrick Toth mentions in his book "Handbook of Paleoanthropology" (Editors: Ian Tattersall, Winfried Henke) that the Ancient Stone Age is ranging from the beginning of Australopithecine's era (2.6 million years ago) to the end of the Pleistocene's era (10,000 years ago).

David Christian commented in his book "Origin Story: A Big History of Everything" that the Ancient Stone Age extended over 95 per cent of the prehistoric times.

Ancient Stone Age: Expansion

The tokens of the Ancient Stone Age were found in many parts of India. For example:

(i) Basin of Soan River in Punjab,
(ii) Chennai of South India.

According to the names of these two ports, one is known as Soan culture and the other is Chennai culture. The tokens of Ancient Stone Age are also found in Sukkur Rai region. Moreover, one finds the tokens of that period in Mirzapur district of Uttar Pradesh, Mysore,

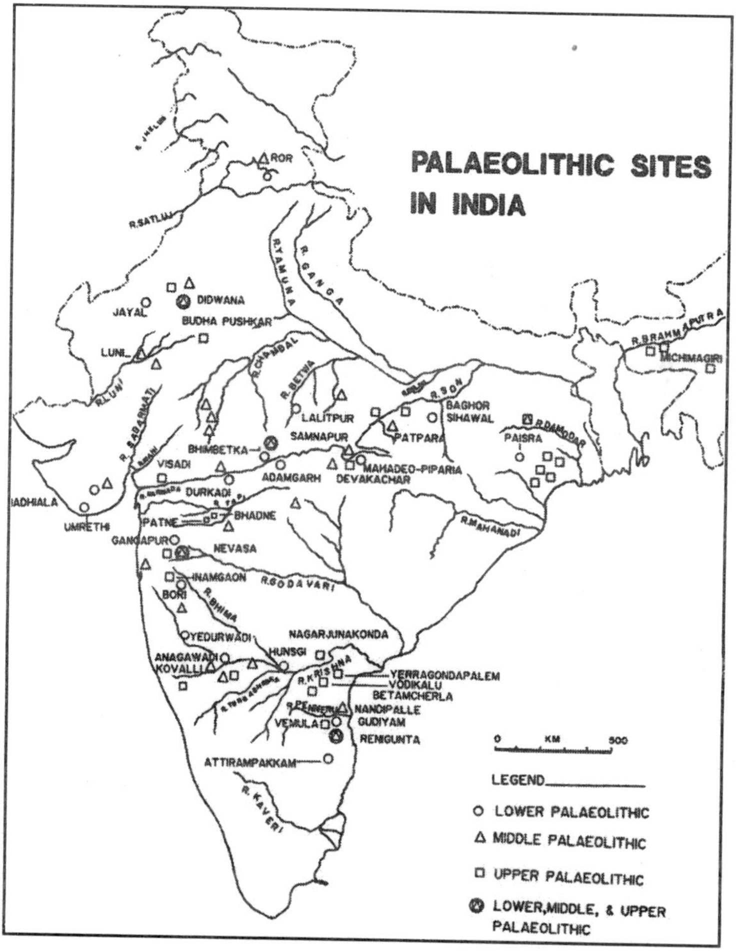

Palaeolithic Sites in India

Tamil Nadu, Gujarat, Ranchi, Hazaribag and in Bankura, Birbhum districts of West Bengal. The Ancient Stone Age at Junagadh district of Gujarat is marked as 1,90,000 years and at Umreth as 69,000 years. The Godavari and Nevasa archaeological sites were more than 4,00,000 years old and Soan River valley of eastern Madhya Pradesh was 1,03,800 years old. The department of Geology of India got human body evidences at Hathtnora village on 5th December 1982 at the coastal region of Narmada River which is north-eastern part of Hoshangabad city in Madhya Pradesh. On the top of this, the evidences of Ancient Stone Age are found at Lalgarh, Kankrajhor in Midnapore; Hatikheda in Bankura; Maluti, Gandorghat in Birbhum; Basundi in Purulia etc. These evidences are also found in Andhra Pradesh and at the Kutch district in the state of Gujarat.

Mesolithic Age

In his book, "Early India: A Concise History", Dwijendra Narayan Jha mentions the Bhimbetka region in his analysis of the Mesolithic Age. The Bhimbetka region is located 49 km south of Bhopal in Madhya Pradesh. Specimens of Paleolithic and Mesolithic Ages were found in this area. Specimens of Mesolithic Age paintings were found in Pratapgarh, Mirzapur and Azamgarh districts etc. Notable among these paintings were food collection, fishing, human hunting, childbirth, sexual intercourse etc. The Mesolithic Ages spanned approximately 10,000 to 6,000 BC. In this age people learned to use fire. At the same time they learned to tame wild animals. The weapons of this era were small in size. They were around 1 to 6 centimeters in length. For this reason, the Mesolithic Age is also described by many as the 'Microlithic' age. However, the shape of most weapons was limited to 1 to 3 centimeters. It was during this period that social organizations were formed. At that time hunting was the main livelihood of the common people. Agriculture was started towards the end of this era. The earthenware industry developed during this Mesolithic Age.

Mesolithic Era: Expansion

In the Mesolithic era the size of the weapons was quite small. Specimens of such weapons have been found in the coastal areas of Gujarat and Mumbai. Such weapons have been found in the valleys of Godavari and Narmada rivers. The Mesolithic period spread across Bihar, Uttar Pradesh, West Bengal, Andhra Pradesh, Rajasthan, Madhya Pradesh, Karnataka, Tamil Nadu etc. According to Upinder Singh, the Mesolithic period found in the Bhilwara district of Rajasthan dates from about 5417 to 4938 BC. Memoirs of the Mesolithic period dating back to 3000 years before the birth of Jesus Christ have been found in Hoshangabad in Madhya Pradesh, Azamgarh and Langhnaj in Gujarat. Mesolithic specimens have also been observed in various districts of Uttar Pradesh. Notable among the regions are Pratapgarh district and Sarai Nahar Rai region. Patterns of this period are also found in the Baghor region of Madhya Pradesh. The specimens of Mesolithic Age have been discovered in the Indus Valley region to the west, West Bengal to the east of India, and the Tinvelli region of southern India. It is also noteworthy that the evidences were also found in Belan Basin and Chopani Mando region.

Middle Stone Age: Analysis

The people of 'Mesolithic Age' wanted to make their lives a little more comfortable and smooth. As a result, they made some changes in their lives. During this time they tried to use small weapons. The use of arrowheads, stone slabs or small pebbles was common in this era. The weapons of the Mesolithic period were more advanced than those of the 'Stone Age' or 'Paleolithic' period. The livelihood of the people of this period was mainly based on animal hunting and fishing. Notable among the weapons used by the people of this age were:

(a) scythe,
(b) 'Batali',
(c) chisel,
(d) 'Shala' etc.

Pets, buffaloes, sheep, cattle, goats, dogs, etc., are notable among the domesticated animals during the Mesolithic time. Fruits, vegetables, honey were common as food. Bones of turtles, hedgehogs, deer, rabbits etc. have been found. From these evidences of this period found in the Birbhanpur region of West Bengal, it can be inferred that women of the Mesolithic period were interested more in procuring food and fuel. Various pictures of social and daily life are found in the Jawar rock layer of Madhya Pradesh. In the Bhimbetka region of Madhya Pradesh, murals of spears, arrows, bows, elephants, tigers, deer, etc. were also found. In addition, various clothing and jewelry images were found. Pictures of burying a child had been noticed on some of the wall paintings. Naturally, the mourning of the bereaved parents also came up. Nude paintings of Mesolithic people or pictures of people wearing tree bark had also been seen on various murals. It was during this period that the Mongols came to India, and the Caucasians came to West India.

Middle Stone Age: Explanation

Paul Bahan explained the term 'Mesolithic' in his book "The Penguin Archaeology Guide". The word 'Mesolithic' comes from two Greek words. The first Greek word is 'Mesos' which means 'middle'. The second Greek word is 'Lithos' which means stone. Adding these two words gives the word 'Mesolithic', which means 'middle stone'. The Middle Stone Age or the Mesolithic Age is the period between the Paleolithic and the Lower Stone Age or the Neolithic Age. The term 'Middle Stone' was used in some cultural trends in the Indian subcontinent.

Ancient Stone Age: Analysis

Dharmapal Agrawal in his book "The Archaeology of India" analyzed the ancient Stone Age and divided this age into three parts. He named the first era 'Paleolithic Age'. He called the second period the 'Mesolithic Age'. According to him, the third age is the 'Neolithic Age'. The beginning of the Stone Age in India is about 3 million years ago. This era is thought to have ended about 10,000 years ago. In the case of the division of the Stone Age, it is divided into three parts:

(a) Upper Ancient Stone Age,
(b) Middle Ancient Stone Age, and
(c) Lower Ancient Stone Age.

Upper Ancient Stone Age specimens can be seen in Mandsaur and Ujjain in Madhya Pradesh. Historians estimate that these specimens are approximately 31,000 years old. The Middle Stone Age lasted from 40,000 to 10,000 BC. Relics of these two eras are found at

Bhimbetka in Raisen district of Madhya Pradesh. Hand axes were used throughout the Stone Age. Patterns of this hand axe are found in—

(a) Attirampakkam in Tamil Nadu,
(b) Ghataprabha river basin in Karnataka, and
(c) Isampur region in Gulbarga district of Karnataka etc.

The identity of various animals can be found in the Upper Ancient Stone Age. Notable among these are wild boar, chital, hyena, wild cat, wolf, black deer, blue cow, horse, rhino etc. Dharmapal Agrawal in his book "Man and Environment in India through Ages" mentioned the scarcity of discussions about the natural environment of the entire Ancient Stone Age. Upinder Singh asked to pay attention to Azamgarh, Bhimbetka cave paintings and rock wall paintings. The colours in these images are green and dark red. The images include hunters, bison, elephants, tigers, rhinos and dancing people.

Neolithic Age

Panchanan Mitra in his book "Prehistoric India: Its Place in the World Cultures" shows that the quality of life of the common man improved considerably in the Neolithic Age. The period from about 6000 to 2500 BC is marked as the Neolithic Period in India. However, this time span is not the same everywhere in India. In southern and eastern India, this period lasted until 1000 BC. We will now discuss some of the features of the Neolithic Age.

First, all the weapons used in this era were much sharper and subtler than in the previous era. The weapons also looked beautiful, smoother. As a result, their effectiveness increased. Second, it is thought that the little weapons used in this era were made of metal. Thirdly, the people of this era were involved in farming with the help of stone fruits. At this time the use of various things made of stone can be noticed.

Another important feature of the Neolithic Age is the construction of mud houses. The history of digging and sowing seeds is also considered to be one of the features of this era. The search for foodgrains like wheat, barley, buckwheat etc. is found in this era. Patterns of pottery made of clay have also been noticed in this period. The clay pots were painted with different colours. The method of making yarn using cotton can also be noticed in this era. Thus, method of weaving cloth was in vogue during this period. Among the domesticated animals in the Neolithic Age were sheep, goats, cattle, etc. Efforts were also made among the people of that time to build cemeteries for the dead and to do their best to preserve the memory of the dead.

The life of the common man improved so much in the Neolithic Age that it is also called as the 'Neolithic Revolution'. Irfan Habib in his book "Prehistory, People's History of India" (Series-1) says that "the Neolithic people introduced a new type or change in agriculture which was a trend of revolution in terms of time."

Neolithic Age: Expansion

If you want to name one of the oldest centres of the Neolithic Age, it must be Mehrgarh. Here you can find polished stone weapons, axes and various tools. Evidences of this period were found in the northern region of eastern Uttar Pradesh. In this context, it is worth mentioning that the Pandu Raja or Pandu Rajar Dhibi mound in West Bengal and the axe, sword, harpoon etc. obtained from Mahishadal region. Signs of Neolithic settlement can be seen in the Maski and Tineveli regions of southern India.

The civilization of this period spread to—

(a) Balathal,
(b) Silud and
(c) Ahar regions of Rajasthan.

Among the important places of Western Maharashtra are—

(a) Songaon,
(b) Daimabad,
(c) Nasik,
(d) Chanduli,
(e) Nevasa, etc. where the traces of this period had also been found.

Neolithic evidneces were found in Assam, Bihar and Orissa in eastern India. In addition, the Kayatha and Eran regions of western Madhya Pradesh can be mentioned.

Neolithic traces have also been found in the Burzahom and Ghafkral areas of the Kashmir Valley in northern India. The time period of the specimens found in this region is approximately 2500-1500 BC. Evidences of this era have also been found in Karnataka and Tamil Nadu. Traces of Neolithic civilization were also found in Indus and Balochistan.

Neolithic Age: Neolithic Revolution

Anil Kumar Gupta, in his essay "Origin of Agriculture and Domestication of Plants and Animals Linked to Early Holocene Climate Amelioration", cited South-West and South-East Asia as examples of the Neolithic Age. The term "Neolithic Revolution" was used by Vere Gordon Childe in the 1920s. The foundation of the 'Neolithic Revolution' was laid with the idea of revolution in agriculture. The period of the Neolithic Age is referred to as the age of revolution. Compared to the Ancient Stone Age and the Middle Stone Age, this era saw a radical change in the way of life in agriculture and the use of tools. The people of this era started new methods of farming. As a result, there has been a great change in agriculture and in the products produced. Some changes were also noticed in the use of weapons during this period. The tools were made of stone. The stone tools of the previous two eras were uneven and unsmooth. The tools of this era were more refined than that. As a result, the effectiveness of the tool naturally increases. In the Neolithic Age, trees were cut down with the help of smooth stone tools. Smooth spades were used to clear the land and sow the seeds. The sharpening of the spearhead and the front of the arrow made hunting much easier than before. After the grain was harvested, the straws obtained from the land were used as fodder for cattle. Interest in hunting diminished, albeit slightly, as milk and meat were easily available from cattle. In the Neolithic Age, houses were made of clay to store the surplus grains. That's why historian Irfan Habib did not hesitate to acknowledge this era as the 'Neolithic Revolution' as a result of such unprecedented changes in agriculture and way of life.

Neolithic Age: Analysis

In 1865, Sir John Lubbock used the term "Neolithic" in his book, "Pre-historic Times as illustrated by Ancient Remains and the Manners and Customs of Modern Savages". The word 'neolithic' also consists of two separate Greek words. The Greek word 'neos' means 'new'. And the word 'lithos' means stone. The word 'neolithic' is formed by combining these two words. Miles Barkit mentioned four characteristics of Neolithic culture:

(a) Raising cattles at home,
(b) Agriculture,
(c) Smooth stone tools,
(d) Pottery.

In 1860, in Uttar Pradesh, Le May Suriar discovered some weapons and other archaeological artifacts of the Neolithic Age. Specimens of this era were also found in Bellary, South India. The people of that time became accustomed to the use of smooth stones. They also became much more advanced in terms of civilization and culture. In the Neolithic Age, people began to live a controlled life.

The practice of agriculture was introduced during this period. The idea of agrarian revolution was also prevalent during this time for agricultural production. The masses became skilled in agricultural production. The Salem district has the largest number of medieval man-made specimens. The workmanship of the bowls, jugs, pots and flower pots made by the potters here was of high quality. The quality of the clay used by the potters was improved. The use of red and yellow colours in pottery was noticeable. Neolithic potters excelled in creating the body beauty of various males and females. The practice of eating raw meat of animals changed before the Neolithic Age. With the advent of fire, the common people of this age began to eat the flesh of animals. The potter's wheel was invented in the Neolithic Age. The Neolithic people mastered the art of hunting through the invention of arrows and bows. Neolithic arrows and bows were much more effective than in earlier eras. The arrowheads were also smooth. The Neolithic Age saw far-reaching changes in the way people lived.

Copper Stone Age

The 'Neolithic Age' is followed by the 'Copper Stone Age'. In this age people gradually started using copper. At a later time the masses began to mix tin and bronze with copper. Then the stone starts mixing with copper. That is why this era is called the 'Copper Stone Age'. The period from 2000 BC to 700 BC was the period of the Copper Stone Age. All the specimens found in this period are believed to be of between 3000 and 600 BC. Kashinath Narayan Dikshit in his book "Neolithic and Chalcolithic Cultures in Eastern India" discusses the development of this civilization in the regions of Eastern India during the Copper Stone Age. Red and black colours were commonly used in the pottery of the Copper Stone Age. Metal use gradually began after the end of the Neolithic Age. The exact location or region from where this period originated is still not clear. The use of copper was found in northern India towards the end of the Neolithic Age. In his book "History of Bengal", Rakhaldas Bandyopadhyay states that metal objects were made of copper in ancient times. Archaeologists have found traces of stone weapons as well as copper weapons and tools of this period. However, not only copper objects but also stone objects were used by the people of this age. In this context, it is necessary to mention the use of stone garland. Apart from this, people also had a keen interest in textile production in the 'Copper Stone Age'. Detailed identities of blacksmiths and potters can be gained in this age. The use of terracotta or ivory can be seen in this era. Among the domesticated animals of the Copper Stone Age were goats, sheep, cattle and pigs. Camels were also considered as essential animals in this era. The example of eating beef can be noticed in this age. At the same time it was common to eat fish. In this era, it was customary to bury the dead on the floor of the house in the north-south direction. Evidence of burial has been found in Maharashtra. Apart from this, evidences of the Copper Stone Age were also found in various parts of Uttar Pradesh, Andhra Pradesh, Karnataka, Rajasthan and West Bengal.

3 HARAPPAN CIVILIZATION

Details of the Harappan civilization can be found in Sir John Marshall's book, "Mohenjo-Daro and the Indus Civilization", Vol.-I, Vol.-II. The origins of the Harappan civilization can be traced in the book "The Indus Valley (Excavating the Past)" written by Ilona Aronovsky and Sujata Gopinath. In the opinion of Sir John Marshall, "The Indus Valley Civilization or Harappan Civilization is the oldest civilization". According to Will Durant, the Harappan civilization is even older than the Egyptian civilization on the banks of the river Nile. The discovery of the Harappan civilization suddenly revolutionized our concept. The Harappan civilization was called the ancient civilization of Indian history as well as the world history. Indian Archaeologist Daya Ram Sahni of the 'Archaeological Survey of India' discovered the Harappa archaeological site in 1921 as the first city to be discovered in the Harappan civilization. In 1922, another Indian archaeologist Rakhaldas Bandyopadhyay also discovered archaeological relics at Mohenjo-daro. Thus, the discovery of the Harappan civilization proves that there was an ancient urban civilization in India even before the Vedic period. The Indus Valley Civilization is referred to as the Harappan Civilization as the city of Harappan was discovered as the first evidence of the Harappan Civilization. In addition, the first phase of the Indus Valley Civilization was found on the banks of the river Indus, so this civilization is called 'Indus Civilization'.

Origin of Harappan Civilization

There are various theories about the origin of the Harappan

Mohenjo Daro (Mound of Dead)

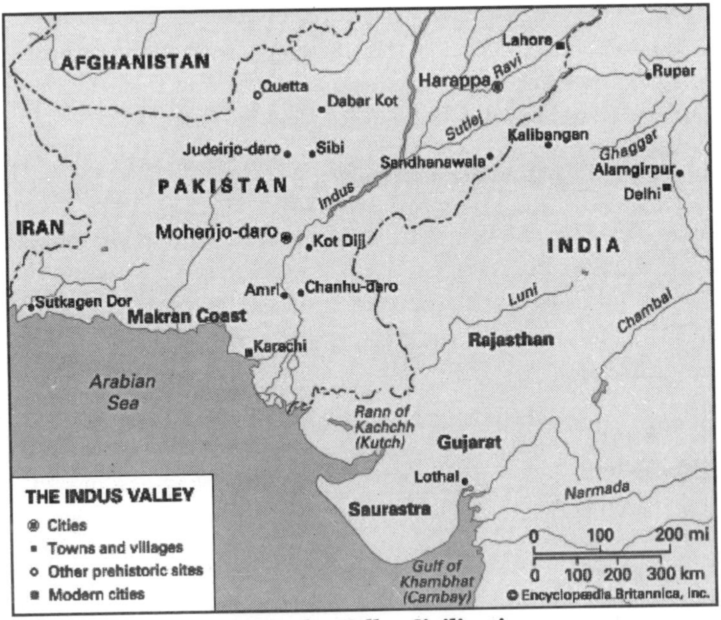

The Indus Valley Civilization

civilization. Stuart Pigot commented on the origin of the Harappan civilization, saying that the Harappan civilization originated within Indian culture. No external force or population worked for the emergence of this civilization. According to most historians, the Harappan civilization dates back to 3000 BC and lasted until 1500

BC. Sir John Marshall found similarities between the Harappan civilization and the Sumerian civilization. On the other hand, Harappan civilization was found to be similar to the Babylonian culture to E. Mackay. Sir John Marshall considered the masses of Harappan civilization to be different from the masses of Aryan culture. Rakhaldas Bandyopadhyay considered the people of Harappan civilization as Dravidians. There are various theories about the origin of the Harappan civilization. Many historians believe that people from Mesopotamia and the Sumerian region entered the cities and towns of Indian civilization. Ropar, located in Satadru (Satlej), was a significant area of Harappan civilization. The spread of Harappan civilization was noticed in Surkotada, Dholavira in Gujarat. The centre of Harappan civilization was discovered at Rakhigarhi in Haryana. The Harappan civilization spread over an area of 1600 km east-west and 1400 km north-south. Most of the Harappan civilization was found in the river basin. The area of expansion of the Harappan civilization was estimated to be about 12,50,000 square kilometers.

Harappan Civilization: The Creator

Scholars differ on the origin of the Harappan civilization. Stuart Pigot thinks that the Harappan civilization was not created by any foreigners. The Indians were the creators of the Harappan civilization. Among the Indian people, the creators of the Harappan civilization are identified as:

(a) Asura,
(b) Brahui,
(c) Dravidian,
(d) Nag, and
(e) Das etc.

There are two theories as to the origin of the Harappan civilization. The first theory is Aryan theory and the second theory is 'non-Aryan' or Dravidian theory. According to Aryan theory, the Aryans were the creators of the Harappan civilization. The Aryan or Vedic civilization was the later civilization of the Harappan civilization. The period from 1500 BC to 650 BC can be identified as the period. If the Aryans are the creators of the Harappan civilization, then it must be admitted that the Aryans came to India in 3500 BC or even earlier. But so far no information has been found to support this view. There are many other theories as to why the Aryans were not the creators of the Harappan civilization. First, the Harappan civilization was a city-centred civilization. But Aryan civilization was a village-centred civilization. Second, in the Harappan civilization, the dead were buried. In Aryan civilization, the dead were cremated. Third, the people of the Harappan civilization did not know the use of iron, but the people of the Aryan civilization were familiar with iron. For the above reasons, there is no logic to consider the Harappan civilization and the Aryan civilization as the same civilization. The Brahui people living in Balochistan can be identified as Dravidian-speaking. In the pre-Aryan period, most of the people of India belonged to the Dravidian group. Many historians believe that there are good reasons to consider the Dravidian nation as the creator of the Harappan civilization. The Dravidians lived in Punjab and Balochistan. According to Rakhaldas Bandyopadhyay, the Dravidian group, the creators of the Harappan civilization, helped in the emergence of the cities of the Harappan civilization. Sir Robert Eric Mortimer Wheeler supported this view. V. Gordon Childe also believed in this same doctrine. Some doctrines were also found against this doctrine. Such an opposing doctrine is: The Harappan civilization originated for the benefit of the native culture or under the influence of the native culture. Indigenous peoples or patrons of indigenous culture have long contributed to the emergence of the Harappan civilization. Arthur Llewellyn Basham was a supporter of this view. Frank Raymond Allchin attributed the emergence of the Harappan civilization to the influence of native or local culture rather than foreign influence. According to Suniti Kumar Chatterji, the Dravidian-speaking people of the pre-Vedic period helped in the emergence of the Harappan civilization. Rakhaldas Bandyopadhyay had the same opinion.

The Spread of Harappan Civilization

Historian Ram Sharan Sharma thinks that there was no great civilization like the Indus Valley Civilization until two or three hundred years before the birth of Jesus Christ. The spread of this

Indus or Harappan civilization was not limited to the Punjab or the Indus region. In addition to the Indus region, it happened in different parts of Gujarat, Rajasthan, Balochistan and western Uttar Pradesh. Apart from Harappa and Mohenjo-daro, the features of Harappa and pre-Harappa civilization were found at Kalibangan in northern Rajasthan, Banwali in Haryana, Chan-hu-daro in Sind province, Lothal in Gujarat. According to Ranabir Chakravarti, the Harappan civilization extended northwards to the Shortugai region of Jammu. To the south, this civilization spread to the Daimabad region of Maharashtra. The western part of the Harappan civilization was Sutkagan Dor in Balochistan and the easternmost part was Alamgirpur on the banks of the Hindu river in Meerut district. The geographical boundaries of the Harappan civilization were quite wide. This civilization extended as far as Jammu in the north. This civilization extended to the mouth of the river Narmada in the south. The civilization spread westwards as far as the Makran coast of Balochistan. This civilization spread as far as Meerut in the east. The spread of the Harappan civilization can be traced far beyond the regions in which civilization developed in Egypt and Mesopotamia. According to Dr. Vasudeva Sharan Agrawal, the Harappan civilization spread from the Saraswati-Satadru (Satlej)-valley along the Indus to Saurashtra. That is to say, calculations show that the Harappan civilization spread over one-third of India. In terms of numbers, this area was 1/2 million square miles. The spread of Harappan civilization was observed from Rupar in Ambala district to Bhagatrav on the Kim River. Suniti Kumar Chatterji also supported this point of view. But there is no suitable evidence as to whether the Dravidian race was the creator of the Harappan civilization. Examination of various human skeletons in the Harappan civilization showed that the region was inhabited by a mixed race. The identities of the two nations found in this region were found:

(a) Mediterranean,
(b) Proto-Australoid.

But no evidence of the presence of the Nordic group or the Aryan group was found. This is why there is a lack of information about the creator of the Harappan civilization. It is not possible to know who the creator of Harappan civilization was without deciphering the Harappan inscription.

The Period of Harappan Civilization: Antiquity

Regarding the period of Harappan civilization, Sir John Marshall, a scholar of Indian archeology, commented in 1931 that the estimated period of Harappan civilization was 3250-2650 BC. The Mesopotamian civilization was contemporary with the Indus civilization. The commercial relationship of the Harappan civilization with Mesopotamia can be traced. This is why Sir John Marshall identified this period as the period of the Harappan civilization. Jane Mclntosh, in her book "The Ancient Indus Valley: New Perspective", discusses the period of the Harappan civilization and identifies the period of evolution of the Harappan civilization as 2700-2500 BC. However, it is not possible to say exactly about the period of the Harappan civilization. Dr. C.J. Gads traces the period of the Harappan civilization to 2350-1770 BC, based on John Marshall's estimates. Stuart Pigot discusses the relationship of Harappan civilization with Mesopotamia and Persian civilization and identifies the period of Harappan civilization from 2500 to 1500 BC. Initiatives were taken to determine the period of the Harappan civilization based on the radiocarbon dating or radiocarbon-14 or C-14 method. Sir Mortimer Wheeler, in his book "The Indus Civilization", took the initiative to mark the period of Harappan civilization. According to Dr. Henry Frankfurt, the Harappan civilization has seven layers or nine layers, dating back to 500 years. He analyzed the Harappan seals and dated it to 2700 BC. That is, the Harappan civilization began in 2600 + 500 = 3300 BC. Historian Will Durant writes, "The Indus Valley Civilization was older than that which flowed out of the mud of the Nile." John Marshall was the first to use the term Indus civilization. Dr. Dharmapal Agrawal identified the period of Harappan civilization as 2300-1750 BC through radiocarbon-14 test. According to Raymond Allchin and Bridget Allchin, the period of the Harappan civilization was limited to 2100-1600 BC. According to Nisha Yadav, the period of development of the Harappan civilization was 2600 BC and the period of decline was approximately 1900 BC. In recent studies, according to Italian archaeologist Paolo Biagi, the period 3000 BC has been identified as the period of the rise of the Indus Valley Civilization or Harappan Civilization. However, there is a problem in determining the period of Harappan civilization. Because we do not have an acceptable time period attested by radiocarbon method. That is why we have not been able to accurately identify the period of the Harappan civilization.

Urban Features of the Harappan Civilization

Jonathan Mark Kenoyer, in his book "Ancient Cities of the Indus Valley Civilization", discusses the urban features of various cities of the Harappan civilization in Pakistan and western India from 2600-1900 BC. Among the cities of the Harappan civilization, Harappan and Mohenjo-Daro were the two main cities. Small towns like Chanhudaro and Alamgirpur also existed. Irfan Habib commented in his book, "Indus Civilization: A People's History of India 2", that one has to look at the cities of Harappa and Mohenjo-Daro to know how the cities of the Harappan civilization developed. Harappa and Mohenjo-Daro are called twin cities because of their similar urban planning. The main feature of the cities of the Harappan civilization was that the cities were divided into two parts.

(a) Elevated area or citadel or fort type and
(b) Low area.

The forts were made of bricks, located on high terraces. These were isolated from the main city. As a result, water would not enter the forts even if it was flooded. The ruling class lived here. The common people lived in the lowlands. There were ramparts around the highlands and arches were found in many areas. There was extra protection in the highlands or trenches around. One-room houses or two-room houses can be seen in the Harappan civilization. People lived in one or two rooms. In the urban life of the Harappan civilization there were:

(a) baths,
(b) drainage system,
(c) roads, and
(d) buildings etc.

The Great Bath

The Great Bath has been discovered at Mohenjo-Daro in the Harappan civilization. The Great Bath was 29 feet long, 23 feet wide and 6 feet deep. Two types of baths were found in the Harappan civilization.

(a) House and bath house in own houses,
(b) Large bath house for the general public. The great bath at Mohenjo-Daro were notable examples of the Harappan civilization.

The great bath at Mohenjo-Daro are 180 × 108 feet. Looking at the depth of this bath house, it seems that there were swimming arrangements here. It had open veranda on three sides. Then there were rooms. Looking at the small rooms around the bath house, it is assumed that the women used these rooms for changing clothes and decorating. The bath house had a brick well in a room for water supply. Nowhere else in the world has such a large bath house been discovered. According to Achut Dattatraya Pusalker, the first lipstick was found in Chanhudaro. It is very surprising that the women of this age knew the use of lipstick. After bathing, the women of Harappan and Mohenjo-Daro used to decorate various ornaments. They used to do hair styling.

Drainage System

The wonderful aspect of the Harappan civilization is the drainage system or sewerage system. In the large cities of the Harappan civilization, houses had drainage and sewerage. The houses were drained by large drains and small drains connected to them. This improved type of drainage system was found in almost all the cities of the Harappan civilization. There was a sewer to get the dirty water out of the house. Covered sewers or underground sewers beside wide roads were a sign of advanced urban civilization. According to Arthur Llewellyn Basham, such patterns were found in Roman civilization also. But no such civilization can be found in any other civilization except the Harappan and Roman civilizations.

Roads

Wide roads were one of the hallmarks of the urban life of the Harappan civilization. The main roads were in many cases connected at equal angles to each other. In the cities some roads were up to 34 feet wide. The narrow lanes were up to 9 feet wide. Small roads and alleys were also found. Houses of equal size were built keeping equal distances on both sides of the road. The urbanization of the Harappan civilization lasted from 2350 BC to 1750 BC.

Building

In the Harappan civilization, buildings were found at relatively high altitudes. But these buildings were not used as homes. The tall and huge building at Mohenjo-Daro is believed to have been reserved for priests. The huge square room of this building is assumed to be the auditorium. The 250-feet-tall building in Mohenjo-Daro was thought to be the ruler's palace.

Harappan Civilization: Class Division

The existence of class division was noticeable in the Harappan civilization. Damodar Dharmananda Kosambi believes that classification existed within the urban layout of the Harappan civilization. The highlands of Harappan and Mohenjo-Daro were inhabited by economically prosperous people. Barnacles, baths or buildings were found in those highlands. The rich and influential lived in the highlands, whereas the lowlands were inhabited by the relatively poor. According to Dwijendra Narayan Jha, one and two-room houses were the earliest condition of the coolie line of modern Indian cities. Thus, Harappan was inhabited by people of rich class on one hand and the poor class on the other. Vere Gordon Childe discussed the context of the classification of Harappan civilizations. According to Mortimer Wheeler, the priesthood was predominant in Harappan society. The priests were the ruling class. Apart from this, in the Harappan social system there is a clear idea about the position of (a) merchant class, (b) peasant, and (c) working class. But it is not possible to accurately determine whether there was class division or class inequality.

Harappan Civilization: Economics

Gregory Possehl discusses the food culture of the Harappan civilization in his book "Indus Valley: Entry from the Encyclopedia of Food and Culture". Agricultural economics was important in the economic field of the Harappan civilization. Agriculture or agrarian living was one of the main features of the Harappan civilization. Agriculture was developed as the economic basis of the Harappan civilization. As the Harappan civilization was based on agriculture, there was no problem in supplying food to the cities of the Harappan civilization. Surplus production from agricultural production was sent to different parts of the city. Wheat and barley were found in Kalibangan, Mohenjo-Daro, Harappa and other areas. Kalibangan and Lothal were notable for grain storage. The use of granaries for storing surplus grain was one of the features of the Harappan civilization. The Harappan granary was 169 feet long and 135 feet wide. The Harappan granary was located on the banks of the Ravi River to facilitate the transportation of food grains by river.

Livestock

The Harappan civilization had the use of livestock for agriculture and food needs. A large number of animal bones were found in the Harappan civilization. The Harappan civilization is believed to have had the presence of bulls from the seals. In the Harappan civilization, domesticated animals were bulls, sheep, buffaloes, pigs, cats, goats, sheep, camels, etc. Dogs were seen as a favourite pet. Camels and donkeys were used for carrying burden. The masses of this civilization were probably not familiar with horses. In western India, bones obtained from Surkotada are considered to be horse bones. But Joyner's research shows that it was the bones of a wild donkey. One-horned quadruped was identified in the Harappan seals. But there are doubts as to whether it was real or not, although elephants are believed to have been in the Harappan civilization.

Technical Industry

One of the economic features of the Harappan civilization is the use of technical industries. Patterns of utensils made of stone and metal were found in the Harappan civilization. In the Harappan civilization

(a) copper and bronze knives,
(b) fishing rods,
(c) batali,
(d) axe,
(e) sickle, and
(f) saw patterns were found.

Copper mirrors were found in Chanhudaro. The people of Harappan civilization used earthenware for their daily needs. Potters used to make pots of different colours. The use and design of red and black colours in glassware, which is as shiny and smooth as glass, was an expression of the skill of the potters. Mohenjo-daro and Harappan weavers were skilled in cutting cotton and wool yarns and making textiles. Iron was not used in the Harappan civilization. In the Harappan civilization, ivory needles, ivory items, copper and bronze mirrors with wooden handles, rice husks were found in seals and clay pots. From which it is inferred that rice was produced in the Harappan civilization. Patterns of various mustard seeds and seeds, sesame and *pigeon pea* were found in the Harappan civilization. The cloth found in Mohenjo-daro was made of corpus. Agriculture was fertile in the Harappan civilization. Because of the floods every year, the silt accumulates and maintains the fertility of the soil. In the economic field of Harappan civilization:

(a) agrarian system,
(b) technical industry, and
(c) trade and commerce were important. At that time raw and burnt bricks were used in construction.

Agricultural System

In his book "Indus Civilization: A People's History of India-2",

Irfan Habib commented that the urban revolution of the Harappan civilization required sufficient agricultural production. In the case of agriculture, water was available from raw and ripe wells. The Harappan civilization was a pioneer in the use of water for cultivation. The people of Harappan kept themselves busy in cultivating two types of crops.

(a) Rabi grains: Mustard, Redlentils, Yellowlentils, wheat, cotton etc.
(b) Kharif grains: Sorghum, cotton, buckwheat, paddy, sesame etc.

Not all regions of the Harappan civilization had rice yields. Kalibangan in Rajasthan shows traces of ancient agriculture in the pre-Harappa period. Hugh Trevor Lambrick thinks that there were two types of crops grown in Kalibangan. There is disagreement as to whether the plow was used in the Harappan civilization. According to Damodar Dharmananda Kosambi, the plow was not used in the Harappan civilization. But hoe was used. It was not possible to cultivate much with the help of hoe.

Harappan Civilization: Granary

One of the features of Harappan civilization was the granaries at Harappan and Mohenjo-daro. These barns were large in size. The granaries were made of burnt bricks. The number of granaries was 6. Grain was stored in granaries. Inside the barn on the banks of the Ravi River in Harappan are two rows of platforms. The presence of 6 additional platforms for storing grain in each row can be noticed. The platform inside these barns is 50 × 20 feet in size. The space between the two rows was 23 feet wide for travel. The granaries had adequate ventilation. The large granary of Harappan had the presence of skilled craftsmen in the manufacture of pottery made of grain storage stone and bronze. The people of the Harappan civilization used stone garlands and steatite stone garlands, copper and lapis lazuli garlands.

Expansion of Business Trade

C.J. Gadd discovered 24 seals from the Ur region of Mesopotamia.

From this seal it is known that Mesopotamia had trade relations with the Harappan civilization. According to Shikaripura Ranganatha Rao, maritime scholars believe that the port of Lohal in Gujarat was a pioneer in maritime trade. Looking at the pictures of ships in the seals found in the Indus region, it can be indicated that there was maritime trade in the Harappan civilization. The merchant community stamped the goods to make sure of their weight and the right thing. All the goods produced in the Harappan civilization met their own needs as well as traded with the contemporary civilization. Shereen Ratnagar remarked that the commercial speed of the Harappan civilization increased due to the exchange of raw materials.

(a) Sapphire or Lapis Lazuli used to come from Badakhshan region of Afghanistan.
(b) The source of copper was the Khetri Nagar region of Rajasthan.
(c) Precious stones came from Cornelian Saurashtra i.e. West India.
(d) Jade used to come from West Asia.
(e) The conch used to come from Rann of Kutch.

The seals obtained from the Harappan region were important means of trade and commerce. Many goods were sent to Sumer from the Meluhha (Melukhkha) region of the lower Indus Valley, such as:

(i) *Onyx*,
(ii) *Baiduryamani*,
(iii) Small figurines of birds,
(iv) Housing wood,
(v) Gold,
(vi) Ivory etc.

According to Ranabir Chakravarti, the seals of the Persian Gulf region were found in Lothal to maintain trade. In addition, the metal used by the artisans of the Harappan civilization was imported from other distant lands through commercial transactions. Internal trade is found in different regions of the Harappan civilization. In case of commercial transactions, Uttar Pradesh, Gujarat and Rajasthan can be mentioned. The Harappan civilization had trade relations with Sumerian, Crete, China, Egypt, Afghanistan, Persia and other civilizations.

Harappan Civilization: Cultural Life

The statue of a naked dancer found in Mohenjo-Daro is one of the cultural lives of the Harappan civilization. The mesmerizing appeal of the smiling faces and eyes of the naked female figure introduces the Harappan art culture. Multiple bronze animal sculptures of the Harappan civilization were the epitome of sculpture. In addition to stone and metal sculptures, terracotta bulls, elephants and mother idols were found.

The people of the cities of the Harappan civilization used weaving and woolen garments. Men and women used to wear separate clothes to cover the upper and lower parts of the body. The hairstyles and ornaments of the women can be identified from the statue of the dancer of Mohenjo-Daro. Among the ornaments of women,

(a) rings,
(b) bracelets,
(c) bangles,
(d) pendants,
(e) anklets,
(f) necklaces etc. were important.

Toy patterns were also found in the Harappan civilization. The people of the Harappan civilization were educated as their seals and inscriptions carry the identity of their signature. Harappan inscriptions were carved in steatite stone. Though these scripts have not yet been deciphered. After long research by Asko Parpola and Iravatham Mahadevan, it was learned that the Harappan scripts were written from right to left. If it is possible to decipher the inscriptions of the Indus Valley Civilization, then something new can be learned about the cultural life of this civilization.

Harappan Civilization: Religious Beliefs

Debiprasad Chattopadhyaya thinks that the religious beliefs of the

Harappan civilization can be deduced from the images in the seals of the Harappan civilization. Although it is not possible to know completely about religious beliefs based on Harappan seals alone. Most of the terracotta statues in the Harappan civilization are female. From this it is inferred that mother worship was prevalent in the Harappan civilization. Naked female idols are more common in the Harappan civilization. It seems that women were seen as a 'symbol of fertility'. According to Dr. Dilip Chakraborty, a seal found in Harappan showed the origin of the tree from a woman's vagina, indicating the fertility of a woman. According to John Marshall, this image was a replica of the goddess '*Shakambhari*'. In a seal, a tiger, an elephant, a rhinoceros, a buffalo and a deer - these five animals are surrounded by a three-faced meditative figure. The statue has two horns on its head. Many people think it is *Shiva* idol, as in Hindu concept, the head is *Trimukh*, *Pashupati* and *Yogeshwar*. Professor Arthur Llewellyn Basham calls it '*Adi Shiva*' because Shiva's vehicle is a bull, but there is no bull in this idol. *Shiva* was also worshiped as the god of fertility. According to Mortimer Wheeler, excavations in the Harappan civilization yielded many terracotta female statues. The crowns of these statues were spread out like 'pekham'. And if you examine the two bowl-like parts on both sides, you can see the burn marks. Mortimer Wheeler thinks that these burn marks came from burning something like incense or those were used as lamps. In fact there was a ritual relationship with these idols. According to the archaeologist Gordon P. Watts, many idols were painted in the Harappan civilization. The Harappan civilization is believed to have had a tradition of smearing vermilion on idols, as in modern times. Since these idols were of gods and goddesses, it was customary to paint them. In the Harappan civilization, 'totem worship' or inanimate objects like trees, animals, stones, etc. were worshiped as gods and goddesses. Naked female idols of the Harappan civilization are considered to be an alternative to mother idols. Bull and snake worship was practiced in Harappan. In addition to mother worship, Harappan civilization includes—

(a) Shakti worship,
(b) Linga worship, and

(c) Vaginal worship. The Indus people believed in life after death. They used to bury the dead. This tomb was of three types—
   (a) Furniture, ornaments etc. were given along with the corpse. It is called full tomb.
   (b) Only the skeleton of the deceased was buried.
   (c) The corpse was cremated and only the remains were filled in a container and buried. Bodies were usually laid from north to south of the cemetery.

The Difference between Harappan Civilization and Vedic Civilization

In his book "Hindu Nationalism, History and Identity in India: Narrating a Hindu Past under the BJP", Lars Tore Flaten discusses the issue of religion in relation to the Harappan civilization and the Vedic civilization. But there is a difference between Harappan civilization and Vedic civilization.

(a) The Harappan civilization was the Copper Age civilization. Ornaments and weapons made of copper and bronze were notable specimens of this period. Other metals such as tin, copper, bronze were used in the Harappan civilization but iron was not. The use of iron was especially seen in the Vedic civilization.

(b) Harappan civilization was more ancient than Vedic civilization. At present radiocarbon tests have identified the period of the Harappan civilization as approximately 2350-1750 BC. But the period of composition of Rigveda is about 1500 BC. So the Harappan civilization is more ancient than the Vedic civilization.

(c) The Harappan civilization is thought to have been city-centred by its baths, well-planned roads, drainage system, buildings, etc. On the other hand, the Vedic civilization was a rural civilization. The main livelihood of the Aryans was agriculture and animal husbandry.

(d) Although traces of other animals were found in the Harappan civilization, no traces of horses were found. The horse skeleton found at Surkotada was identified by Joyner as the skeleton or bone of a wild donkey. But horses existed during the Aryan period.

(e) The people of Harappan civilization were associated with trade and commerce. In the case of Vedic civilization, although they were farmers, they were not so accustomed to trade and commerce. They made their living by raising animals.

(f) War-centred mentality is found in the period of Vedic Aryans. In the case of the Harappan civilization, war-centric issues are not found. The people of the Harappan civilization chose a peaceful civic life.

(g) Harappan civilization had the use of inscriptions or seals. Lots of seals were discovered in the Harappan civilization, though the inscriptions on the seal could not be deciphered. But seals or inscriptions were not found in the Vedic age. Vedic literature was based on myths and memories.

(h) Bodies were buried in Harappan civilization. Excavations at Harappan resulted in the discovery of many tombs, but the Vedic Aryans cremated corpses.

(i) There were also religious differences between the Harappan and Vedic civilizations. In Harappan civilization bull was worshiped. Cows were worshiped in the Vedic period. In the Harappan civilization, '*Pashupati*' or '*Adi Shiva*' was worshipped in seals. In the Harappan civilization, besides trees and animals, the mother goddess was worshiped. Male deities were predominant among the Aryan deities. The Vedic Aryans used to spend more time in Yajna. The practice of Yajna is not found among the Harappan people.

(j) In Harappan civilization, the colour of pottery was red and black. But in the Vedic period gray pottery was used. Thus, there were cultural differences between the two civilizations. No images were found in the pottery of the Vedic Aryans. However, pottery was depicted in the Harappan civilization. This is why Sir John Marshall identified the Harappan civilization and the Vedic civilization as separate civilizations.

The Causes of the Decline of the Harappan Civilization

Nayanjot Lahiri in his book "The Decline and Fall of the Indus Civilization" thinks that there is a controversy about the fall of Harappan or Indus civilization. There are two theories about the decline of the Harappan civilization.

(a) Natural causes,
(b) External causes or attacks. Shereen Ratnagar in his book. "The End of the Great Harappan Tradition" (2000), discussed the theory that the Harappan civilization collapsed as a result of external aggression.

According to Dharmapal Agrawal, the Harappan civilization did not exist until after 1750 BC. Dr. Irfan Habib also commented that the existence of the cities of the Harappan civilization was suddenly no longer visible. Seals, pottery, bronze utensils, etc. were no longer found in the Harappan civilization. The decline of the Harappan civilization was revealed in the book "Indus Civilization" edited by R.K. Pruthi, who said that the Harappan civilization collapsed in 1700 BC. Natural disasters were blamed for the collapse of the Harappan civilization. On the other hand, the statements of Mortimer Wheeler etc. suggest that the Harappan civilization collapsed due to the attack of an external enemy.

Natural Disasters: Earthquakes

Earthquakes were mentioned in the fall of the Harappan civilization in the book 'Indus Civilization' edited by R.K. Pruthi. Excavations in the Harappan civilization have shown after analyzing the soil layer that the Harappan civilization collapsed as a result of earthquakes at various times. In Mohenjo-Daro, many skeletons were found piled up and mutilated. Skeletal scars were also noticed and were not buried. As a result, many historians consider the claim of seismic theory to be appropriate. According to Hasmukhlal Dhirajlal Sankalia, the city of Mohenjo-Daro was destroyed about seven times but they have rebuilt it. However, seismic theory cannot be accepted because it is not known whether earthquakes occurred everywhere in the Harappan civilization.

Flood

Evidence of floods is found in the Harappan civilization. The Indus Valley region was prone to floods. At least three catastrophic floods have been reported in Mohenjo-Daro. As a result, Mohenjo-Daro was destroyed. According to the writings of George Wells and Rycom, the region was damaged by the flooding of the Indus River. The floods destroyed the Harappan civilization. According to M.R. Sahani, "Flood may have swept the Indus Culture". But other areas of Harappan civilization like Harappan, Lothal, Kalibangan, Banwali, Ropar etc. did not see floods. On the contrary, Hasmukhlal Dhirajlal Sankalia said that Kalibangan was destroyed as a result of drying up of the Ghaggar river. Thus, forestry cannot be blamed for the collapse of the Harappan civilization.

Economic Reasons

The two reasons for the decline of the Harappan civilization were

(a) loss of trade, and
(b) non-expansion of agriculture.

Economic factors or economic crisis was one of the reasons for the downfall of the Harappan civilization. Agriculture did not extend from the Indus Valley to the fertile Gangetic Valley as the people of the Indus Valley were not familiar with iron and ferrous materials. It was not possible to expand in agriculture using tools made of iron like plows and axes. Lack of dams in the Indus Valley weakened the irrigation system and prevented the expansion of agriculture. It was not possible to expand agriculture by clearing forests with the help of iron tools. Although the population has increased, agricultural production has not increased. The decline in the quality of goods in the Harappan civilization led to a decrease in the amount of goods exported. The trade exchanges between the Harappan civilizations and the civilizations of West Asia were gradually declining. Irfan

Habib commented in his book "The Indus Civilization: A People's History of India-2" that the commercial exchange of the Harappan civilization with Mesopotamia had ceased. 'Economic stagnation occurred in agriculture and trade. The result was the fall of the Harappan civilization.

Climatic Change

Climate change can be cited as a natural cause of the decline of the Harappan civilization. According to Mortimer Wheeler, burnt bricks were used to build houses for urbanization in the cities of Harappan or Indus. For this, the local forest was cut down and the wood required for burning bricks was collected. As a result, many trees were cut down. This process of deforestation reduced rainfall. Many areas of the Harappan civilization became deserts. The Harappan civilization collapsed due to lack of water due to declining rainfall. According to Hungarian archaeologist Sir Marc Aurel Stein, the Indus Valley region gradually dried up after the Copper Stone Age. As a result, the upper part of the farmland became white, dry and brittle. This kind of aridity in the land was the cause of the downfall of the Harappan civilization. Although it is not possible to say with certainty whether the areas of the Harappan civilization except the Indus fell by this analysis, many historians believe that the decline of the Harappan civilization was inevitable when the Indus and the Satadru (Satlej) and Jamuna rivers once changed their course. Due to lack of irrigation in different places, the agricultural system collapsed abruptly. The problem could have been solved by digging a canal, but the people of Mohenjo-Daro did not go that way, they probably left the city and went elsewhere. According to Hasmukhlal Dhirajlal Sankalia, the flood was caused by a change in the course of the Indus, which destroyed the civilization. But no argument can be found for this theory unless the course of rivers in cities other than the Indus changes.

Conservative Mentality

Although the Harappan civilization reached the pinnacle of excellence in many ways, it could not improve and update itself with the times.

The Harappan civilization could not learn anything from the Egyptian or Sumerian civilizations in order to hold on to the old. Many historians believe that this conservative mentality was the cause of the destruction of the Harappan civilization. Firstly, the rulers of the Harappan civilization could not accept the positive aspects of other contemporary civilizations. Mesopotamia developed agriculture for improved irrigation systems. The masses of the Harappan civilization had no interest in knowing or learning it. Secondly, although the Indus Valley civilization had commercial dealings with West Asian civilization, the Harappan people did not learn advanced agricultural equipment and techniques for making heavy weapons. This conservative mentality of the masses of the Harappan civilization was negative. Thirdly, the lack of a sense of urbanization was also a factor in the decline of the Harappan civilization. According to Mortimer Wheeler, the archaeological remnants found later in Mohenjo-Daro and Harappan was a reflection of their former appearance. Fourthly, despite the gradual decline in foreign trade, the people or rulers of the Harappan civilization did not seek any alternative. Fifthly, the people of Harappan did not feel the need to dig canals for irrigation. Sixthly, they did not think of building heavy weapons to protect themselves from the attacks of other nations. Many historians believe that the Harappan civilization collapsed because of the conservative mentality described above.

Theory of External Aggression

Guy D. Middleton, in his book "Understanding Collapse: Ancient History and Modern Myths", provides information on the decline of ancient civilizations. There are many exaggerations in that information. There are natural causes as well as theories of external aggression in the fall of the Harappan civilization. Excavations in various parts of the Harappan civilization have unearthed skeletal remains in many areas. Signs of injuries were found in the skeletons. Skeletons were also found on the streets, on stairs or in bathrooms. No signs of burial were found in the skeletons except for sharp weapon wounds. Dwijendra Narayan Jha, referring to all these examples, remarked that in Harappan there was a battle between the non-

Aryans and the foreign Aryans in 'Hariyupia' which resulted in the fall of Harappan. According to historians such as Mortimer Wheeler and Damodar Dharmananda Kosambi, the Harappan civilization collapsed as a result of foreign invasions or Aryan invasions. According to the Rigveda, the Aryan deity Indra was identified as Purandara or the destroyer. Indra took the name 'Purandar' after destroying the cities of Harappan civilizations. The period of the fall of the Harappan civilization and the arrival of the Aryans is almost the same which is approximately 1500 BC. That is why the connection between the two events can be noticed. An axe made of copper and bronze found in Chanhudaro bears a resemblance to an Iranian axe. Therefore, since the Aryans came to India on their way to Iran, many consider it an axe to the Aryans.

External Attack: Evaluation

There is disagreement about the cause of fall of the Harappan civilization, whether it is because of the external invasion, or of the Aryan invasion. According to archaeologist Hashmukhlal Dhirajlal Sankalia, the discovery of corpses as a result of an enemy attack on the Harappan civilization was different from that of the Harappan civilization. Skeletons of human beings were found in the Harappan civilization in different parts of Asia. According to archaeologist Ernest John Henry Mackay, the attackers are believed to be residents of Balochistan. According to Ram Sharan Sharma, no evidence of conflict between the people of the Harappan civilization and the Aryans was found. So, the theory of Aryan invasion was based on conjecture. Natural factors, economic factors, the nature of the mentality of the citizens were largely responsible for the decline of the Harappan civilization. According to John Marshall, natural disasters are considered to be one of the main reasons for the decline of the Harappan civilization. Mortimer Wheeler's theory of Aryan invasion was considered an exaggeration in the fall of the Harappan civilization.

4 VEDIC AGE AND IRON AGE

Before the discovery of the Harappan civilization, the Vedic civilization was thought to be the earliest period of Indian civilization. But this idea changed after the discovery of the Harappan civilization in 1921. There are several differences between the Harappan civilization and the Vedic civilization. The period in which the Rigveda was written is considered to be the period of the Rigvedic civilization.

The period of composition of the other three Vedas, namely *Sama Veda*, *Yajur Veda* and *Atharva Veda* is identified as the later Vedic age. In his book "An Outline of the Aryan Civilization", Ramendra Nath Nandi discusses many aspects of the earliest period of Vedic civilization i.e. the Rigvedic period. He also sheds light on the meaning of the word 'Aryan' in this book. B.B. Lal commented that the Vedic civilization is the successor of the Harappan civilization. He further said that Vedic civilization can also be called Aryan civilization as Vedic civilization was created by Aryans. But who are the Aryans? There is a difference of opinion among the scholars as to whether they are from India or not.

The Word 'Aryan': Linguistic Viewpoint

Friedrich Max Müller, the German-born philologist and orientalist scholar, thinks that 'Aryans' do not really mean any ethnic group. The people who used Aryan language are called 'Aryans'. He added that at the scientific level, the word 'Aryan' can never be used in a racial sense. No word other than language was called 'Aryan'. According to Sir William Jones, the founder of the Asiatic Society of Bengal, Aryan is the name of a language group. The Sanskrit language of India has a deep connection with the major languages of the Indo-European language group, including Greek, Gothic, and Latin, commented Filippo Sassetti. Following this idea, Sir William Jones also said that Sanskrit was a branch of the Indo-European language group. In Vedic Sanskrit, the word Aryan was not used in a racial sense. To linguists, Aryan is the name of a language group. This language group is Indo-European. Indo-European languages are: (1) Greek, (2) Iranian, (3) Sanskrit, (4) Latin, (5) German, and (6) Slav etc.

Aryan Word: From the Point of View of Race

If taken literally, the word 'Aryan' means 'descendant of honest and good family'. The word 'Aryan' was used in the nineteenth century in India in a racist sense to establish the dominance of Hindus and Hindu civilization. At that time the tide of nationalism came to our country. The reason was to oppose British imperialism. Darius was the emperor of Persia about 500 years before the birth of Jesus Christ. He called himself of 'Aryan descent'. The word 'Aryan' originated in English in the racial sense. Hitler, the dictator of Germany, identified the descendants of the Nordic nation as 'Aryans'. According to Jaskacharya, the non-literal meaning of the word 'Aryan' is 'child of God'. That is, the righteous Son of God is called 'Aryan'. A verse in Sanskrit language says. Those who are knowledgeable and those who go beyond the limits of studying the scriptures, they are 'Aryans'. Bhimrao Ramji Ambedkar thinks that the word 'Aryan' was never used in the Vedas to mean 'race'. There the language of the two human groups was considered as 'Aryan'. (1) Palpine is a pre-Aryan race belonging to the human race. (2) The Aryan race of the Vedic age recognized as the Vedic Brahmins belonging to the Nordic human race. Thus, it is reasonable to explain the Aryan race in terms of linguistic group or linguistics.

The Original Habitat of the Aryans: A Debate

Exactly where the original abode of the Aryans was is still a mystery. The main reason for this controversy is the scarcity of archaeological evidence of the time. As a result, historians rely solely on linguistic

Religion in Later Vedic Period

Weapons in Vedic Age

analysis. The analysis through which researchers and scholars have sought to determine the original habitat of the Aryans is largely based on conjecture. According to a group of scholars, India was the original home of the Aryans. Notable among these scholars are D.S. Trivedi, Ganganath Jha, A.C. Das, B.B. Lal and others. According to another group of scholars, the original abode of the Aryans was not India at all; they came to India from somewhere else. Important among these followers are Dr. B.K. Ghosh, Wilhelm, Brandestein, P. Giles and others.

Origin of Aryans: India

Sanskrit has similarities with Latin, Celtic, European and German. This similarity proves that Aryans are not Indians, they are foreigners. That's what Trottman thinks. But—

(a) Ganganath Jha thinks that Vedic Sanskrit was the source of language and literature in India. Therefore, India is the original home of the Aryans.

(b) According to L.D. Kalla, the original habitat of the Aryans was the northwestern Terai region of Kashmir and the Himalayas. Many historians have suggested that the region on the banks of the Devika River in Multan was inhabited by Aryans. Notable among the supporters of this same opinion are D.S. Trivedi, Ganganath Jha, A.C. Das *et al.*

(c) Saptasindhu or seven rivers is mentioned in Rigveda. As a result, many historians have suggested that the Aryans were from the Saptasindhu region of Kashmir, Multan or the Punjab. S. Trivedi thinks that Multan is considered to be the original residence of the Aryans.

(d) Another view is that Aryans are Indians. Because all the trees and animals mentioned in the Aryan literature and Vedic literature can be seen in India.

(e) The name of any country other than Saptasindhu is not found in Vedic literature. As a result, many historians believe that the Aryans are the people of India. Otherwise, the mention of the country from which the Aryans came would have been reflected in their literature.

(f) F.E. Pargiter thinks that there is no evidence that the Aryans came to India from the north-west. But it was possible for the Aryans to move out of India from the north-west. The name of the rivers mentioned in the river hymns of the Rigveda took the name Ganga in the east and Saraswati in the north-west. This river hymn proves that the Aryan race traveled from east to north-west.

(g) There is no reliable archaeological evidence to support the fact that the Aryans were outsiders.

(h) According to D.S. Trivedi, Multan was the original abode of the Aryans. Although L.D. Kalla thinks that Kashmir and the Himalayas were the original habitats of the Aryans.

(i) In many cases different Indian languages originated from Sanskrit but no effect was seen on European languages. For that reason it can be assumed that the pre-Vedic language was the language of the Aryans. Other Indo-European languages were created as a result of the migration of Aryans from India to other countries and their relations with other non-Aryan groups.

(j) Archaeologist Sir Marc Aurel Stein commented in his journal 'The Geographical Journal' that the Saraswati River began to dry up around 3000 BC and became completely extinct around 2000 BC. Seeing the repeated mention of Saraswati in the Rigveda, it seems that the period of its composition is even before the Indus civilization. But this idea is not justified. This is because the Harappan civilization developed before the Aryan civilization and the repeated mention of the river Saraswati in the Rigveda identifies India as the original abode of the Aryans.

(k) Swami Vivekananda in his book "The East and the West" (Prachya O Paschatya) introduced the subject of Vedic literature and opposed the theory that Aryans came from outside India, commenting that, "The original home of the Aryans is believed to have been in India".

(l) But according to Andrew Colin Renfrew, "nowhere in the Rigveda is it mentioned that the Aryans were outsiders." It seems that the Aryans settled in India long before the composition of the Vedas.

(m) Dr. Subhash Kak identified the original abode of the Aryans as India.

Ganganath Jha commented on the original habitat of the Aryans in India. Brahmarshidesh was a region of five rivers extending up to Mathura. This region was the original home of the Aryans. D.S. Trivedi also thinks that the Multan and Devika river areas were the original home of the Aryans. Pandit Lakshmidhar Shastri thinks that the Himalayan hills were the original abode of the Aryans. The Aryans first settled in the Himalayas. Rajbali Pandey mentioned Madhya Pradesh, situated between the Saraswati River, Prayag and Vindhya region, as the original abode of the Aryans. In his book "Rig Vedic India", Dr. A.C. Das referred to the Saptasindhu region as the true abode of the Aryans. The Saptasindhu (Sapta Sindhavah) region was bounded on the north by the Kashmir Valley and on the west by Gandhara. According to him, the seven rivers

(a) Sindhu (Indus),
(b) Vitasta (Jhelum),
(c) Asikni (Chenab),
(d) Parushni (Ravi),
(e) Vipasha (Beas),
(f) Satadru (Sutlej) or Satudru, and
(g) Saraswati river region i.e. 'Saptasindhu region' was the original abode of Aryans.

According to Navrath Rajaram, James Safar, SP Gupta, David Fradley, Georg Feuerstein, etc., India was the original homeland of the Aryans.

The Original Habitat of the Aryans: External Theories

(a) Astronomer Rajesh Kochhar has scientifically analyzed the book 'Vedanga Jyotisha' and found that the ratio of the longest day to the shortest night in this book is 3: 2. The probable location of the region with such features could be 35 degrees north axis. No region other than Shortugai (Shortughai) of the Harappan civilization alone is situated on this high axis. Thus, the Aryans as a whole were not Indians, but non-Indians or foreigners. Edward Meyer referred to the southern region of Central Asia as the original home of the Aryans. Ernst Herzfeld thinks that the vast plains of the two rivers Amu Darya and Syr Darya were the original home of the Indo-Iranian Aryans.

(b) McDonnell said that the Eastern Europe was the original homeland of Aryans. Two inscriptions were discovered in Asia Minor and Egypt.
   (a) Boghaz Koi,
   (b) Tell-el-Amarna,

(c) The Boghaz Koi inscription discovered in Asia Minor, inscribed in 1400 BC, mentions the names of Vedic deities such as Indra, Mitra and Varuna. In the inscription called Tell-el-Amarna discovered in Egypt, the names of the kings of Syria are similar to the names of the Aryans. Analysis of these aspects suggests that the Aryans lived in this region before coming to India.

(d) According to J.C. Rodd, Bactria was the original habitat of the Aryans.

(e) According to A.L. Basham, the nomadic peoples who lived in the grasslands from Poland to Central Asia during about 2000 BC were the ancestors of the Aryans who came to India.

(f) According to the historian Hart, the Aryans crossed the Caucasus Mountains from Europe and entered Persia. From there they started their journey towards India.

(g) According to American Historian Paul W. Schroeder, Info-European-speaking peoples originally lived in the grasslands of southern Russia. P. Giles identified modern-day Hungary, Austria, and Bohemia as the original home of the Aryans.

(h) Lokmanya Bal Gangadhar Tilak in his book "Ancient Home of the Vedas" thought that the Arctic region or the North Pole region was the original home of the Aryans. From this region they settled in the central region.

(i) Dr. P. Giles and Professor MacDonnell linguistically said that the Aryans were originally from modern Austria, Hungary and Bohemia. They noticed that the flora and fauna, which were known to the Aryans, were found only in temperate regions.

(j) The famous Vedic scholar and founder of the Aryan society, Dayananda Saraswati in his book "Satyarth Prakash" and the foreign scholar Frederick Eden Pargiter in his book "Ancient Indian Historical Tradition" called Tibet the original abode of the Aryans.

(k) Dr. B.K. Ghosh in his book "The Vedic Age" identified the Aryans as outsiders. Five of the seven languages in the Indo-European language group were European. The Sanskrit language group moved from Europe to India.

(l) Among the currently prevalent European languages, the Lithuanian language is related to the main features of the Indo-European language. Lithuania is located between Eastern and Western Europe. That is why the European Aryan language group is believed to have originated in Lithuania.

(m) If India was the original home of the Aryans, then the Aryans would maintain their dominance over the whole of India. But Aryan culture did not spread all over India or South India.

(n) Wilhelm Brandenstein commented on the original homeland of the Aryans, that the original homeland of the Indo-European peoples was the Kirghiz Steppe (Kazakh Steppe) or vast grasslands of present-day Russia.

From that region, one group crossed Asia Minor to Europe and the other to Iran. After a short stay in Iran, a group of them entered India through Afghanistan. The other group remained in Iran. Thus, according to Wilhelm Brandenstein, the Kirghiz grasslands south of the Ural Mountains in Russia were the original home of the Aryans. In his book, "The Problem of Aryan Origins", K.D. Sethna argues that India was the abode of the Aryans. On the other hand, he also argues on detail and discusses various logics as to why Aryans were not the inhabitants of India. The Aryan problem or the controversy over the original habitat of the Aryans still exists. In recent times, the nearly 7,000-year-old temple in the Gobekeli Tepe region of Turkey and the symbol of relief found in Ukraine have given a new lease of life to Aryan history.

Rigvedic Era: Political Situation

At the Rigvedic period, the political and social basis of the Aryans was the patriarchal family. According to Ram Sharan Sharma, the head of the family was called 'Kulapati'. The basis of the political system at that time was the village—this is the opinion of the historian Romila Thapar. At that time the villages were formed with a few families, a vish was formed with a few villages. A Jana was made with a few Vish. The head of the Vish Vas called 'Vishpati'. In Rigvedic period, the head of the village was called-Gramani. The head of the Jana was called 'gop' or 'king'(Rajan).

Foundation of the State: King

Historian Romila Thapar refers to the king as a military leader or war leader during the Rigvedic period. At that time the throne was hereditary. The king was elected. The king, however, claimed to have divine powers. His main task was: (1) to protect the country from external enemies, (2) to punish the offender, (3) to protect the property of the tribe. There were (1) Gramani, (2) Senani, and (3) priests to help the king.

Gramani, Senani, Priests

In the Rigvedic era, those who were the rulers of the village were called 'Gramani'. They also had the responsibility of maintaining peace and order in the village. The role of 'fighter' was in the military field. They fought with the help of cavalry and infantry. In the Vedic age, the job of the 'priest' class was to act as the king's advisor. They were also able to influence the king. In the Rigvedic age (a) Vishwamitra, and (b) Vashistha was the political adviser of the king.

Sabha, Samiti, Vidath

In the Vedic age, the 'Sabha' was the council of elders or the council of tribal chiefs. The 'Sabha' had the power to decide on any important matter. The 'Sabha' also played an important role in the subsequent trial. D.M. Apte commented in his book "The Vedic Age" that dice were played here and rich people were present. The role of 'Samiti' was much more important than that of 'Sabha' in the Rigvedic era. The 'Samiti' was made up of the elite and the masses. The king used to participate in the sessions of the 'Samiti'. The 'Samiti' had the right to instruct the king about his duties. It is understood that the 'Samiti' was much more powerful and representative. 'Vidath' was the Constituent Assembly. Various political issues including war were discussed here. In this Constituent Assembly, with 20 members, the king used to distribute the wealth collected and plundered by the war.

Rigvedic Era: Social Condition

The society of the monotheistic era was basically patriarchal. The leaders of the family or group were all men. They were called 'Grihapati' or 'Kulapati'. Only the oldest men in the family were elected as head of the family. Though patriarchal importance was almost prevalent at that time, still daughters were not neglected by parents. Women had the freedom to choose their husbands. The instances of widow marriage have also been found since that era. In the Rigvedic age, the relationship between all the members of the family was very close. There is an example of a widow marrying brother-in-law after her husband's death. The Rigveda mentions Yami's proposal of marriage to his brother Yama. In that era, there was no division between men and women in religion. There is no mention of Sati or child marriage. Outside of marriage, male-female relationships were maintained. Sukumari Bhattacharya commented that there was no problem in the society with this.

Rigvedic Society: Caste Discrimination and Class System

Damodar Dharmananda Kosambi, in his discussion on monotheistic society, said that there was no class or ethnic discrimination in the society. But there was class division in the society on the basis of white Aryans and black non-Aryans. In the tenth mandala of the Rigveda, 'Purusha Sukta', four castes were mentioned. Brahmins were born from the mouth of the Brahma, Kshatriyas were born from his arms, Vaishyas were born from his navel and Shudras were born from his feet. In addition to this caste system, four different classes of responsibilities were observed on the basis of action.

(a) The work of Brahmins was to do the religious practices.
(b) It was the duty of the Kshatriyas to defend, fight and rule the country.
(c) It was the duty of the Vaishyas to conduct agriculture and trade.
(d) It was the job of the Shudras to serve these three classes mentioned above.

According to Ramsharan Sharma, the word 'Varna' was used to distinguish between black non-Aryan and fair Aryans. Romila Thapar thinks that there were three classes in the monotheistic society.

(a) Kshatriya: elite or warrior class,
(b) Brahmin: priest class, and
(c) general class. In the later period a fourth class called Shudra emerged. There were no barriers to marriage between different classes. For example, sage Chyavana was married to Kshatriya Sukanya.

Rigvedic Era: Women

Sukumari Bhattacharya remarked that there was a clear mention of women's freedom in the Rigvedic era. Shashwati, Visvavara, Ghosha, Apala, Surya and other women even held *Upavita*. They had the right to read the Vedas. As a result, they were called women sages. There was no obstacle for them to participate in the meetings and associations. At one point in the Rigveda, the new widow is being advised to marry one of the survivors and have children. The Rigveda also mentions the issue of temporary intercourse with the brother-in-law for childbearing. Among the deities of the Aryans in the Rigvedic society, the number of goddesses like Ila, Bharati, Saraswati, Bakva, Jsha etc. was more. The number of male deities increased in later times. That is, later the society became male dominated. Outside of marriage, male-female relationships were maintained.

Rigvedic Era: Clothing, Food, Entertainment

In the society of Vedic age, (a) wool, (b) cotton, (c) deer skin was used for clothing. There was no difference between men's and women's clothing. They both wore turbans and wore ornaments. In the Vedic age there were three parts to clothing.

(a) Nivi: The underwear that is used in the lower part.
(b) Adhivasa: Used for upper body.
(c) Angrakha: long dress. There are many identities of women's hairstyles.

D.M. Pandey mentioned milk and ghee as the staple food of the Rigvedic era. Vegetables, fruits, dairy products, meat were also one of the staple foods of the Aryans. In addition to beef, the Aryans ate sheep, goats, and bulls. But dairy cows were not killed. The amount of beef eaten later declined. The consumption of alcohol is also mentioned in Rigveda. D.S. Pandey termed alcohol as polite destroyer and atheist in the society of the Rigvedic era. In the Vedic society there were daily pleasures like

(a) hunting,
(b) boxing,
(c) dance songs,
(d) recitation,
(e) hymns etc.

According to Dr. Arthur Berriedale Keith, drama was also prevalent in the Rigvedic era, which was the earliest genre of drama dialogue in India. There was a horse race between the amusements. Gambling, dancing and going to brothels were also common as part of entertainment.

Rigvedic Era: Economic Condition

Hemchandra Roychowdhury spoke on the economics of the Rigvedic age, in which pastures were the property of the common people. Ecology and arable land were privately owned. Romila Thapar said the land was initially owned by the village. Later, as tribal organizations gradually weakened, land was allotted to village families. Thus, private ownership was created. In the Rigvedic age, there were two bases of economy:

(a) agriculture and
(b) animal husbandry. According to Romila Thapar, Aryans were pastoralists during the Rigvedic period.

Then they concentrated on agriculture. Agriculture and animal husbandry was their main livelihood. Paddy and barley were cultivated during the Rigvedic period. Cattle were the main animal husbandry. The word 'gavishti' means to search for cows. 'Gavishti', the sanskrit word for 'war', literally translates as 'desire' for more cows. Horses were used to transport grain. Land and waterways were equally important for trade in the Rigvedic era. The technical industry was also prosperous in the Rigvedic era. Weaving and pottery were in vogue. In the Rigvedic age, 'nishka' was identified as a medium of exchange, which was probably a 'gold coin'. A coin called 'Mana' was also found.

Rigvedic Era: Religion

During the Rigvedic period, two ways of practicing the religious activities were observed. (a) Yajna: The fire of Yajna was considered to be the source of immortality of the gods. Ordinary people used to try to fulfill their desires with the help of Yajna. Sacrifices were performed to please the gods. Yajnas were performed on the altar. The king used to organize this sacrifice. Ghee and offerings were offered on the altar with offerings and various mantras were recited to the deities. There were two types of sacrifices.

(a) Nitya: Agnihotra was Nitya Yajna. This yajna was performed by lighting fire, reciting mantras, and adding ghee to the fire.
(b) Casual: This yajna was organized for a special purpose in a particular season.

Sacrifice was another aspect of the Aryan religion. The importance of this sacrifice in the religious field was immense. Sacrifices were arranged in the family or after receiving something from God. Sacrifice was a religious matter. But the festival was organized through sacrifices. There were drinking arrangements. Yajnas and sacrifices were performed under the supervision of Brahmin priests.

Rigvedic Era: Gods and Goddesses

In the Rigveda, Devaraja, the king of gods, Indra was the most powerful of the gods. He used to kill demons with lightning. In the Rigveda, Indra was called 'Purandara' or the destroyer of the city. Purandara is given as a name of Indra as destroyer of stongholds. Most of the hymns of the Rigveda are dedicated to him. Varuna as the deity was 'Dharitri brata', meaning the one who holds everything. He was also the keeper of the order of the universe. He was the keeper of all natural and unnatural laws. Agni was the priest of the gods. He was the one who accepted the offerings made to the gods. Rudra was the god of destruction. Indra was called 'Vajrayudha'. Mitra was the god of keeping oaths and promises. The sun was the god of light, Yama was the god of the dead, Marut was the god of storms, Vayu was the god of wind and Parjanya was the god of rain. In the time of Rigveda, the earth was the god of the earth and Dyaus or Dyauspitar was the god of the sky. In the early days of the Rigveda, the earth was considered to be the mother and the Dyaus to be the father. Vishnu is not given much importance in Rigveda. Among the goddesses Aditi, Arundhati, Pushan and Usha were notable.

Rigvedic Era: Political Situation

The power and influence of the king increased in the later Vedic period. The king was awarded various titles. Such as:

(a) Sarbabhumi,
(b) Ekrat,
(c) Emperor,
(d) Universal etc.

The main aspects of the king's power were Ashwamedha and Rajasuya Yajna. In the Vedic age, large kingdoms emerged instead of small kingdoms. The Yajurveda reflected aspects of a king and his constitutional powers. In order to be a skilled king in the field of governance,

(a) he has to provide food regularly;
(b) he has to be highly educated and experienced. He has to create a religiously minded upper class.
(c) Must have a good army and a skilled commander in charge of the army.
(d) The grievances of the people should be heard and their needs should be met easily and quickly.
(e) Security of life and property must be protected.
(f) Efficient governance should be developed.
(g) To build honest, disciplined and educated civil society.
(h) It is necessary to maintain quality trade.

Dr. A.S. Altekar called meetings and associations a powerful political definition. If the association had taken a destructive attitude in any case, the condition of the king would have been deplorable. In the later Vedic period, the power of the king increased but the importance of meetings and associations decreased. The king could not become an autocrat because the meetings and associations were controlled by rich people and Brahmins. In the later Vedic age there was 'Bhagdugha' (collector of taxes) or tax collector. Apart from this,

(a) Bali,
(b) Bhaga and Bani,
(c) There was an employee named Grahi Tri for collecting revenue.

In addition, the king's messenger called 'Palagala', 'Ritru' or the principal of the royal inner city, 'Sut' or chariot driver, 'Akshavapa' or the principal of Axis sports or Accountant. The identity of the 'Sovikrata' or the Minister in charge of the forest etc. is found. In the later Vedic period, in the village administration, the 'architect' was in charge of the tribal areas, the village ruler was the villager, the occupied village level government servant, the 'Ugra' was in charge of peacekeeping in the village and Shatapathi was in charge of one hundred villages. The existence of 'Vairajya' or republic can be noticed in the later Vedic age. There are five types of state system during Vedic period which is given:

1. Rajaya (Central Kigndom): Ruled by Raja
2. Bhojya (Southern Kingdom): Ruled by Bhoja.
3. Swarajya (Western Kigdom): Ruled by Svarat.
4. Vairajya (Northern Kingdom): Ruled by Virat.
5. Samrajya (Eastern Kingdom): Ruled by Samrat.

Rigvedic Era: Social Condition

In the later period of the Vedas, in addition to the four castes, the names of many new castes can be known. These castes include blacksmiths, fishermen, carpenters, tanners, etc. The condition of the Shudras was the most deplorable. They were considered untouchable and unclean. During this time the caste system gradually became birth-based. Conflicts between Brahmins and Kshatriyas continued. The number of Shudras increased. At this time (a) two communities called Bratya and (b) Nishad were noticed. The two communities were collectively called 'Chandals'. The severity of caste discrimination was especially evident in the later period of the Vedas.

Later Vedic Age: The Position of Women

The status of women declined in the later Vedic period. During this period there were Brahmabadini women like Gargi and Maitreyi. But they were the exception. There were various restrictions on the religious conduct of women. Evil practices such as child marriage and gambling were seen in the society. As a result of polygamy, the dignity of women was greatly diminished. The upper caste women lost the right to recite the Vedas and Upavita. The age of marriage for women was reduced. Women began to live under the father in childhood, husband in youth, son in old age or widowhood. Women's freedom declined in the later Vedic period. At the time of Yajurveda, it was said in the scriptures, "Just as a piece of cloth is wrapped around a stick in a yajna, so a man will be supported by two women. But no woman can support two men."

Later Vedic Age: Clothing, Food, Entertainment

D.M. Pandey commented that it is known from *Satapatha Brahmana* that a type of footwear made of pig skin was used at this time. Both men and women wore silk garments. Clothing made from sheep's wool and goat's wool was worn. In the *Satpatha Brahmana*, emphasis was placed on the wearing of clothes and garments. There was also a demand for colourful clothes at this time. The use of 'prakash' or metal ornaments, 'shalali' or comb and conch can be seen. At this time woolen garments 'Urnasutra' were popular. There is mention of rice cooking in the later Vedic period. In *Satpatha Brahmana*, there is a topic of cooking 'paramanna' or payes by mixing milk and rice. In addition to vegetables and fruits, yogurt, butter and honey are mentioned in the later Vedic period. Soma Ras Alcohol was popular at this time.

Later Vedic Age: Economic Conditions

N. Jayapalan, in his book "Economic History of India", commented that there are descriptions in Vedic literature about the economics of the later Vedic period. Wheat and barley production was seen in the later Vedic period. In case of production in agriculture, there is evidence in *Satpatha Brahmana* (a) plowing, (b) sowing, and (c) harvesting at home. Ramsharan Sharma spoke of sharp edge of plow made of iron in the later Vedic age. This kind of plow was used to clear the forest. In the *Atharva Veda* and in the *Satapatha Brahmana* there is a mention of a plow drawn with twenty-four oxen. During this time cotton was produced. Buffaloes were used for agricultural purposes. Irrigation methods and fertilizers were applied in agriculture. In the later Vedic period, Rajgir, Gaya, Vaishali, Sravasti, Delhi, Mathura and Takshashila (Taxila) were identified as trade routes for the transport of industry and trade. Internal and external trade flourished in the later Vedic period. Goat skins and textiles were traded. A hill tribe called Kirat used to give clothes and leather in exchange for *Mriganavi* and herbs. People of various professions were found in the later Vedic period. Such as:

(a) physician,
(b) dancer,

(c) chef,
(d) Fuller (washarman),
(e) jeweler merchant,
(f) weaver,
(g) potter,
(h) interest trader,
(i) chariot driver,
(j) flute player,
(k) carpenter,
(l) weaving artist,
(m) color mason etc.

In the later Vedic age—

(a) Nishka or Nishk (gold coin),
(b) Satamana, and
(c) Krishnala coins were in circulation. It is assumed that the merchant community formed organizations among themselves. In addition to gold, copper, silver, and bronze, tin, iron, and lead were used. The use of (a) buffalo, (b) sheep, (c) goat, (d) horse and (e) cattle was notable among the domesticated animals during this period.

Later Vedic Age: Religious Atmosphere

In his book 'Vedic Civilization' Raj Pruthi, while discussing the religion of the Vedic age and its atmosphere, raised the subject of gods and goddesses like Savitri, Agni, Indra, Vishnu, Surya, Mitra, Varuna, Usha etc. But in the later Vedic age the status of gods like Indra, Agni etc. was somewhat diminished. Brahma, the creator of the living world, had the highest status. The status of Rudra or Shiva increased. In the later Vedic age, the complexity of Yajna increased enormously. The Brahmin community took the responsibility of conducting the Yajna as the highest priest. Hotri mantra was chanted to invoke deity. Uddhasatri used to sing *Samveda* and recite mantras with the help of Adhburya book. Romila Thapar commented on the subsequent Vedic age, when the forest-dwellers and the abandoned masses sought an alternative to the Indian style. It is known from

Aranyaka and Upanishads that the main goal of the Vedic Aryans was to attain 'salvation'. Salvation is liberation from the bondage of birth and death. In the Aranyaka it was told how to be liberated through meditation and in the *Atharva Veda* it was told how to attain liberation by taking sannyasa. Ramsharan Sharma saw the Upanishads theory of the mingling of man's soul to the supreme soul of god Brahma as the philosophical basis of the people's allegiance to the monarchy. The complexity of philosophical theory increased during the later Vedic period. The Upanishads discussed (a) Brahma, (b) Atma, and (c) Public relations with God and issues of religious ideology. The Upanishads spoke of action, maya, liberation and rebirth. Rudra or Shiva and Vishnu became more important in the later Vedic age.

Iron Age: India

In her book "The Painted Gray Ware: An Iron Age Culture in Northern India", Vibha Tripathi discusses the Iron Age culture in northern India. The period during the prehistoric period when metal weapons and equipment were made of iron was termed as the 'Iron Age'. This prehistoric period is divided into three parts in terms of archeology:

(a) Stone Age,
(b) Bronze Age, and
(c) Iron Age.

The duration and features of the Iron Age varied from region to region. Extensive use of iron was found in the Vedic period. It is believed that the Aryans first started using iron. The use of iron is an important event not only in the history of India but also in the history of the world. The Hittites were the first to use iron in Asia Minor during 1400-1100 BC. Iron was first used in India around 1100 BC. In the Iron Age, three types of cultures developed in the Iron Age:

(a) Painted gray pottery culture,
(b) Northern black pottery culture, and
(c) *Mahasiya* Samadhi culture.

In his book "A Study of Northern Black Polished Ware Culture:

An Iron Age Culture of India", Tribhuvan Nath Roy discusses the features of the black smooth pottery culture of the north.

The Spread of the Iron Age

According to Rakesh Tiwari, the history of metallurgy in India dates back to the second century BC. The spread of the Iron Age was seen in different parts of India. Archaeological sites such as

(a) Malhar,
(b) Dadupur,
(c) Lahore Dewa, and
(d) Raja Nal Ka Tila in present day Uttar Pradesh have found evidence of iron use during the period 1800-1200 BC.

An Iron Age tomb was discovered in the archaeological site of Hyderabad. From the book "Early Antiquity" written by I.M. Diaconoff, it is known that iron was widely developed in India at the beginning of the first century BC. An ironworks was discovered in eastern India in the first century BC. According to the Upanishads, edited by Patrick Alivelle, the use of iron is also mentioned in the Indian Upanishads. The Iron Age spread to different parts of India. R. Tiwari reported by radiocarbon testing that all the Iron Age instruments found in Uttar Pradesh date from 1800 to 1200 BC. The use of iron was observed in the Central Gangetic valley and the eastern Vindhya region. According to Rakesh Tiwari, iron was first used in southern India around 1000 BC. Hallur, Karnataka and Adichanallur were notable among the various regions of South India. The names of Lahuradeva, Kosambi, Jhansi and Allahabad are also found in the Iron Age regions of India. In his essay "Iron Age Burial Site Discover", K. Venkateshawarlu referred to the archaeological finds in Hyderabad as Iron Age tombs. In his book "Early Antiquity", I.M. Diaconoff referred to Mysore in southern India as one of the places of the Iron Age. According to "The New Cambridge History of India" written by J.F. Richards, Gordon Johnson, Christopher Alan Bailey the use of iron was common even in the Mauryan period. N.R. Banerjee, in his book "The Iron Age of India", describes the use of iron in India from the Aryan period onwards. In the book "A Sourcebook of Indian Civilization" edited by Niharranjan Roy and Brajadulal Chattopadhyay, the period of Iron Age in India was seen differently in different regions. But the use of iron was seen in different parts of India between 1000 BC and 500 BC. These important regions include

(a) the upper Gangetic valley and adjoining areas,
(b) the Malwa plateau region and the Tapti valley region,
(c) the South and Central Indian megalithic regions,
(d) the central and lower Gangetic valley regions, and
(e) the northwestern regions, mainly Peshawar region etc. Hastinapur and Atranjikhera were notable among the iron regions of northern India.

Iron Age: Features: Painted Gray Pottery Culture

Even before 1500 BC, various products made of iron were found in

(a) Dadupur near Lucknow,
(b) Ahar of Rajasthan, and
(c) Malhar of the Central Gangetic Basin.

The use of iron gave rise to new towns and cities. Trade and commerce, agriculture and technical industries improved. But gray pottery cultures were found in many parts of western Haryana, Punjab, Rajasthan and Uttar Pradesh. Such pots were smooth and light. Their colour was ash and dark gray. A black design was found on the pot. The painted gray pottery was found at Bhagwanpura, Panipat, Sonepat, Baghpat, Ropar in Punjab, Hastinapur, Ahichatra, Jakhera, Mathura, Sallapur in Uttar Pradesh, Jodhpur, Sarpargarh, Nehi in Rajasthan. Among the iron products found here were

(a) arrow blades,
(b) spear blades,
(c) axes,
(d) knives.

The people who used the painted gray pottery did not use it extensively at first as soon as they learned to use it. The use of iron increases in later times. The period of culture of this painted gray pottery in general was 1100-500 BC. According to B.B. Lal, the Aryans developed this culture. According to Romila Thapar, this culture is in complete harmony with the way of life of the Aryans reflected in the Vedic literature. Agriculture is found in this culture. Iron was also used along with copper, bone and glass. Paddy and barley were the main crops. Cows, horses, pigs, sheep were the domesticated animals of this period.

Iron Age: Northern Black Smooth Pottery Culture

A new type of pottery was found in the Iron Age. This new type of pottery was black and red. They also had designs on them. Iron materials with black and earthenware were found at Mahishadal in West Bengal, Panduraja mound, Sonepur in Bihar, Rajgir, Chirand, Kaushambi in the east of Uttar Pradesh, Rajghat, Prahladpur. Among the iron products

(a) spear blade,
(b) razor,
(c) arrow blade, and
(d) batali were notable.

In his book 'Archeology of Eastern India', D.K. Chakraborty states that the use of iron began in eastern India around 1000 BC or some time before that. Nagel of Gujarat, Broach, Eran, Nagra, Maheshwar, Tripuri in Madhya Pradesh; in Maharashtra's Prakash, Hall and Nevasa, a black pottery culture developed.

Iron Age: Mahashmiya Tomb

Tools made of iron (a) arrow blade and (b) knife etc. were found in Mahashmiya tomb. The mausoleum found at Gufkala in Kashmir dates from 2000 to 1000 BC. There were many different types of tombs. After the corpse was buried, it was surrounded by a round stone. Among the Mahashmiya tombs were Elleswaram in Andhra

Pradesh, Nagarjunikonda, Janapani in Maharashtra, Khapa, Dhanora in Madhya Pradesh, Krashagiri in Karnataka, Halingali. Patterns of Mahashmiya tombs were found in the Malabar region. More than 250 pottery tombs or corpses were buried in one or more containers at a Mahashmiya in Amuthamangalam in Chingalput district of Tamil Nadu, patterns were found. There are Mahasmiya tombs at Maski in Karnataka, Devikulam in Kerala, Dhanora in Madhya Pradesh. Stone and terracotta items were found in the Mahashamiya tomb fields. Apart from this, patterns of gold, silver and bronze items were also found in the Mahashmiya tomb. The period of Mahashmiya Cemetery at Naikunda in Maharashtra is 800-420 BC. The culture of the Mahashmiya period in India was rural culture. The cultivation of wheat, barley, buckwheat, paddy and pulses and the progress of pottery, wood work, and metal industry was remarkable. The monumental tombs found in Jangalmahal and Kotia in Uttar Pradesh were shaped by rural culture.

THE RISE OF THE SIXTEEN MAHAJANAPADAS AND MAGADHA

5

The sixteen Mahajanapadas were formed in the sixth century BC, about the time of Gautama Buddha. These sixteen Mahajanapadas are mentioned in Buddhist literature, as Morgens Harman Hansen states in his book "A Comparative Study of Thirty City State Cultures: An Investigation". Generally, 'Janapada' is a 'locality'. A 'Janapada' refers to the area where a 'Jana' or a particular group had a foothold. That is to say, the settlement of a certain group in a certain area is called 'Janapada'. Historian Hemchandra Roychowdhury has commented that these sixteen Mahajanapadas are mentioned in Jain and Buddhist literature. Jain scriptures "Jain Bhagwati Sutra" and Buddhist scriptures "Vinaya Pitaka", "Sutta Pitaka", "Abhidhamma Pitaka", "Anguttara-Nikaya" etc. are contemporary texts of sixteen Mahajanapadas.

Sixteen Mahajanapadas: Name

In the sixth century BC, the names of 16 Mahajanapadas were found. In his book "Republics, Kingdoms, Towns and Cities in Ancient India", G.P. Singh mentions Anga among the sixteen Mahajanapadas. The names of sixteen Mahajanapadas are found in the Buddhist scripture "Anguttara Nikaya". The names of these sixteen Mahajanapadas are:

MAHAJANAPADAS

(1) Kasi, (Varanasi)
(2) Kosala, (Shravasti)
(3) Anga, (Champa or Cham Panagari)

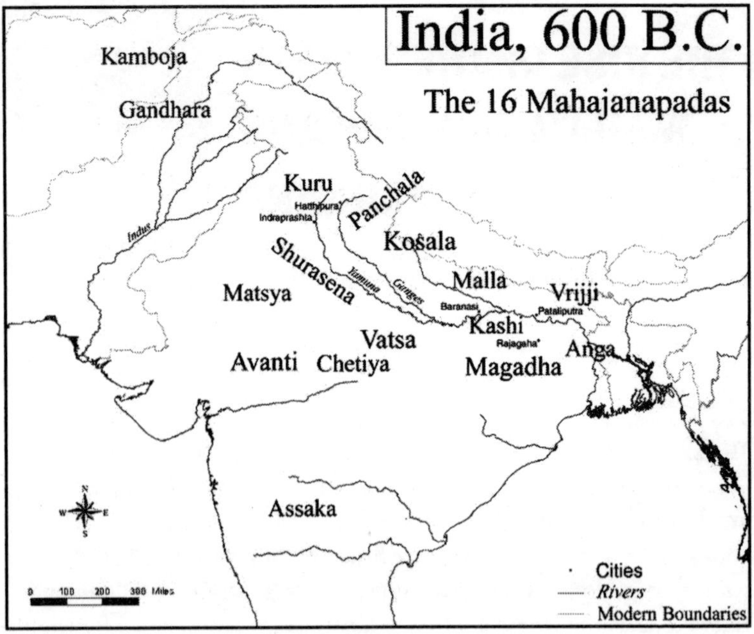

(4) Magadha. (Girivraj or Rajugriha)
(5) Vajji or Vriji, (Vaishali)
(6) Malla, (Kushinagar or Pava)
(7) Chedi, (Suktimati)
(8) Vatsa, (Kaushambi)
(9) Matsya, (Viratanagari or Viratnagar)
(10) Surasena, (Mathura)
(11) Kuru, (Hastinapur)
(12) Panchala, (Ahichchhatra, Kampilya)
(13) Assaka or Ashmaka, (Podana/Potali)
(14) Avanti, (Ujjain, Mahishmati)
(15) Gandhara, (Taxila)
(16) Kamboja. (Rajouri/Rajpur)

There is no mention of 'Gandhara' and 'Kamboj' in the 16 Mahajanapadas mentioned in the Buddhist "Mahāvastu". Instead there is 'Sibi' in Rajasthan and 'Darshaneke' in Madhya Pradesh. The 16 Mahajanapadas mentioned in the Jain scripture "Jain Bhagwati Sutra' are:

(1) Anga,
(2) Banga,
(3) Magadha,
(4) Malay,
(5) Malab,
(6) Sachch,
(7) Batsa,
(8) Kachch,
(9) Rarh,
(10) Pandya,
(11) Bajji,
(12) Malla,
(13) Kashi,
(14) Koshal,
(15) Abah,
(16) Santuttar.

From the names of the 16 Mahajanapadas found in this Jain scripture, it can be inferred that there were more than 16 Mahajanapadas. In the Hindu text "Anguttara-Nikaya", the details of 16 Mahajanapadas were given more importance.

Sixteen Mahajanapadas: Introduction

M.K. Agarwal in his book "From Bharata to India Volume-1; Chrysee the Golden" mentions the introduction of sixteen Mahajanapadas and the existence of sixteen Mahajanapadas in northern India, though 'Assaka' was in South India. The sixteen Mahajanapadas extended from the north-western frontier region to the Narmada-Godavari in the south and from Ujjain in the west to Bhagalpur in the east. Of these, four Mahajanapadas gradually became stronger. These four Mahajanapadas are: (1) 'Magadha' led by Bimbisara-Ajatashatru, (2) 'Kosala' led by Prasenjit, (3) 'Avanti' led by Pradyot, (4) Vatsa led by Udayan. These four Mahajanapadas were of special political importance. Vajji or Vriji also played a special leading role politically. Although Kuru and Panchal, were identified as strong, their importance later declined. 'Kasi' also lost its former significance. Although Kosala was strong at this time, Magadha was the strongest of the sixteen Mahajanapadas. Avanti and 'Vatsa' were defeated near Magadha. 'Magadha' occupied the most important political and imperialist position of the sixteen Mahajanapadas.

(a) Kasi: The area we now know as Benares, in the past this Banaras (Varanasi) was the capital of Kasi. The area was quite safe and secure as Kasi was surrounded by the two rivers Varuna and Aussie.
(b) Kosala: The Kosala region, situated on the banks of the Saryu River, consisted of the Lucknow, Gonda and Faizabad regions of present day Uttar Pradesh. Its capital was Shravasti. Kosala included Kasi in its kingdom. The king of Kosala, Prasenjit, tried to spread the kingdom all over India.
(c) Anga: The Anga Mahajanapada was located in the present Bhagalpur to the east of Bihar. Champa was the capital of this Mahajanapada situated on the banks of the river Champa. According to the Buddhist scripture "Digha Nikaya" ("Collection of Long Discourses"), Champa was one of the six most important cities in India. Earlier during the Haryanka dynasty, Anga was included in Magadha.
(d) Magadha: The most important and powerful Mahajanapada of the sixteen Mahajanapadas is called 'Magadha'. The Mahajanapada was formed in the Patna, Rajgir and Gaya regions of present-day southern Bihar. The first capital of Magadha was 'Rajagriha', the area now known as 'Rajgir'. Pataliputra was the capital of Magadha during the reign of Udayabhadra, the son of Ajatashatru.
(e) Vajji or Vriji: The Vriji Mahajanapada was located in the Muzaffarpur area of present day Bihar. The capital of this Mahajanapada, a republic consisting of 6 tribes, was Vaishali or present day Basri. Notable among the eight tribes which made up 'Vriji' were: (1) Vajji, (2) Videha, (3) Licchavi, (4) Sakya and (5) Jnatrik etc. 'Vriji' was initially a rival of the Magadha Empire but later became part of the Magadha Empire.
(f) Malla: The Malla Mahajanapada, which was formed in the Gorakhpur region of present day Uttar Pradesh, was initially

a monarchy but later became a republic. The capitals of Malla were Kushinagar and Pava. Malla was also conquered by the Magadha Empire.

(g) Chedi: The Chedi Mahajanapada was formed with the present Bundelkhand region. The Chedi were an ethnic group. According to Buddhist scriptures, the capital of Chedi was Shokshibati or Suktimati. In the "*Mahabharata*" its name is mentioned as Shaktimati.

(h) Vatsa: Vatsa Mahajanapada was formed around the present Allahabad region and its adjoining areas. The capital of this Mahajanapada was Kosambi or Koushambi. Udayan was the name of the ruler of 'Vatsa' Mahajanapada. "Kathasaritsagara" contains the account of Udayan's victory.

(i) Matsya: The Matsya kingdom was formed around the Jaipur-Alwar region of present day Rajasthan. The Viratanagari was the capital of this Mahajanapada. In the "*Mahabharata*", the king of Chedi, Sahaj, was mentioned as the lord of fishes.

(j) Surasena: Surasena Mahajanapada was formed around the present Mathura city. The capital name of this mahajanapada is 'Mathura'. Avantiputra is mentioned as the ruler of this region. Greek writers described Mathura as 'Methora'. Megasthenes's "Indica" also mentions Surasena Mahajanapada. During the reign of Chandragupta Maurya, Surasena was included in the Maurya Empire.

(k) Kuru: With the "*Mahabharata*" anecdote, the term 'Kuru' was originally monarchical but later took the form of a republic. This Mahajanapada was formed with present day Delhi and its environs. 'Hastinapur' or 'Indraprastha' was its capital.

(l) Assaka: There is a difference of opinion as to where exactly Assaka Mahajanapada is located. According to Dr. Hemchandra Roychowdhury, this mahajanapada was located on the banks of the river Godavari in South India. According to Bhattasvamin, a commentator on Kautilya's "*Arthashastra*", the Mahajanapada was located in the Maharashtra region. The capital of the Assaka Mahajanapada was 'Podala' or 'Potali', now known as 'Bodhan' in Maharashtra.

(m) Panchala: Panchala Mahajanpada was located in the area between Rohilkhand and Ganga-Jamuna Doab in present day Uttar Pradesh. In the sixth century BC, the Panchala Mahajanapada was divided into North and South. The capital of Uttar Panchal was 'Ahichchhatra' in present day Bareilly district. The capital of Dakshin Panchala was Kampilya in the present Farukhabad district. The Panchala Mahajanapada was transformed from a monarchy to a republican Mahajanapada.

(n) Avanti: Avanti Mahajanapada was located in Malwa and western part of Madhya Pradesh. This Mahajanapada was divided into north and south by the river Betrawati. The capital of North Avanti was Ujjain and the capital of South Avanti was Mahishmati on the banks of river Narmada. It was later incorporated into the Magadha Empire.

(o) Gandhara: The 'Gandhara' Mahajanapada was formed with the Peshawar and Rawalpindi areas of present day Pakistan. The capital of this region was Takshila (Taxila) which was an important learning centre of ancient India. According to the Behistan Inscription, Darius included Gandhara in the Magadha Empire.

(p) Kamboja: Initially a monarchy and later a republican mahajanapada 'Kamboja' belonged to present day Pakistan occupied Kashmir. The ancient Rajouri or Rajpur in the Hazara district of present day Pakistan was the capital of the Kambojas.

Sixteen Mahajanapadas: Monarchical and Republican

Of the sixteen Mahajanapadas, the Monarchical and the Republican Mahajanapadas are identified. Non-monarchical republican moneylenders were also important. Vajji and Malla made their debut as republican mahajanapadas. Kuru and Panchala also gradually became republicans from the monarchical Mahajanapada. The Kambojas also went from monarchical moneylenders to republican moneylenders. During the reign of Magadharaja Ajatashatru, 36 republics of Vajji (Vriji) opposed Ajatashatru. Licchavi was a significant republic during this period. Most of the republics like Vajji (Vriji), Malla, Licchavi etc. were defeated by the Magadha Empire and became part of the Magadha Empire. According to Damodar Dharmananda Kosambi, the republics, despite strong resistance against Magadha, were eventually forced to surrender. Magadha thus became prosperous by defeating various republics. According to Dr. Dwijendra Narayan Jha, the ancient republics and the Malla tribes were weakened by the defeat. Among the important republics of ancient India were: (1) Shakila of Kapilabastu, (2) Kolia of Ramgram, (3) Licchavi of Vaishali, (4) Videha of Mithila, (5) Malla of Kushinagar, (6) Maria of Pipplibun, (7) Allakappar Buli, (8) Malsoi of Montserrat, (9) Oxydracoi of Multan are identified. In addition to the royal mahajanapada, there was a republic mahajanapada in Magadha. These republican states were united against Magadha. The local tribes ruled these republican states. Keshputta's Kalma, Susumagiri's nephew was also a republic.

Magadha Empire: Rise

According to A.L. Basham, the history of India in the sixth century B.C. was able to dispel the uncertainties of its past. Ramesh Chandra Majumdar also thinks that our knowledge of political history was most clear in the sixth century BC. The background of the rise of the Magadha Empire was also created during this time. Out of the sixteen Mahajanapadas, four Mahajanapadas played a leading role in the expansion of political dominance. These four Mahajanapadas are:

(a) Kosala under the leadership of Prosenjit,
(b) Vatsa under the leadership of Udayan,
(c) Avanti under the leadership of Pradyot, and
(d) Magadha under the leadership of Bimbisara and Ajatashatru.

But in the end Magadha established itself as the most powerful of the other Mahajanapadas. Four dynasties contributed to the rise of Magadha:

(1) Haryanka dynasty (545-430 BC),
(2) Shaishunaga (Sishunaga) dynasty (430-362 BC),
(3) Nanda dynasty (362-329 BC), and
(4) Maurya Dynasty (324-187 BC). It is believed that the first empire was established in India under the leadership of

Magadha. The coup d' etat of Magadha as an imperialist power began during the reign of the Haryanka dynasty.

Haryanka Dynasty: Ruler Bimbisara (543-493 B.C.)

In his book "History of Asia", B.V. Rao referred to Bimbisara and Ajatashatru as 'great rulers' among the rulers of the Haryanka dynasty. Bimbisara was the first ruler of the Haryanka dynasty. Atul K. Sinha in his book "Approaches to History, Culture, Art and Archeology" has identified the period from 543 BC to 498 BC as the period of Bimbisara, the ruler of the Haryanka dynasty. Although Upinder Singh commented in his book "A History of Ancient and Early Medieval India: From the Stone Age to 12th Century", the period of Bimbisara was from 545 to 493 BC. The rise of Magadha started from the time of Bimbisara. Upinder Singh thinks that Bimbisara took the title of 'Shrenika' or 'Senia'. It was during the time of Bimbisara that Gautama Buddha attained Bodhi. Bimbisara adopted the imperialist policy. His imperialist policy had three aspects:

(a) Marital relations: Bimbisara increased the power of Magadha through her marital relations with other Mahajanapadas. He married Kosala Devi, the daughter of Koshalraj Maha Kosala and sister of Prosenjit. As a result of this marriage he got Kasi which became a famous pilgrimage site at that time. Kasi was also an important trade center. Bimbisara also married Chellana, the daughter of Chetak, the ruler of Licchavi. As a result, the empire of Magadha spread to Nepal. Bimbisara also married Videha princess Vaidehi. Bimbisara also married Madra princess Khema (Kshema). As a result of the marital relationship, Bimbisara's influence spread far and wide.

(b) War: Bimbisara continued his policy of expanding his empire through war. He fought against the neighbouring state organs. At this time, Kosala and Licchavi were neutral. The conquest of Anga brought the whole of eastern Bihar, including Champa, under Magadha. As a result, Magadha became much more prosperous in terms of trade. According to Dr. Hemchandra Roychowdhury, the conquest of Bimbisara and the expansion of the empire in Magadha began with the conquest of Kalinga by Asoka.

(c) Friendly relations: Bimbisara continued the policy of expansion of the empire through friendly relations. Gandhara's Pukkusati sent envoys to Bimbisara and established friendly relations. He made a friendly relationship with Madra through a marital relationship.

Bimbisara's relationship with Kosala and growth was friendly. Bimbisara established an efficient regime in Magadha. He divided the system of governance into three parts:

(a) the Judiciary,
(b) the Military Department, and
(c) the Administrative Department. The present Rajgir was his capital. There is a common belief that he was killed at the hands of Ajatashatru, the unborn child of the Buddhist hater Chellana.

Ajatashatru (493-462 B.C.)

Historian Upinder Singh discusses the expansion of Ajatashatru's empire. In his time, the rivalry between Magadha and Kosala was intense. As a result, news of the battle of Ajatashatru with Kosala King Prosenjit is also available. Ajatashatru was married to Prosenjit's daughter Vajira and Ajatashatru recaptured Kasi. Magadha's dominance was intact as Ajatashatru won the conflict between Magadha and Kosala. Then 36 republics including 'Vajji' Mahajanapada and 'Lichhavi', 'Vaishali' were involved in the war against Ajatashatru. According to the Jain *Bhagavati Sutra*, 36 republics were united under the leadership of the king of Lichhavi. There was a good relationship between Licchavi and Kosala. Ajatashatru appointed two administrations, Bossakar and Sunidha, to create conflict between empires like Vajji. The title of Ajatashatru was 'Kunika'. He used two weapons during the war with the republics which brought him success. The first is 'Mahashila-Kantaka'. The second is 'Rathamusala'. This 'Mitra Sangha' was formed with 9 Lichchhabi rulers under the leadership of Vajji, 9 Malla rulers under the leadership of Malla and 18 tribal rulers of

Kasala-Kosala. Ajatashatru won the war against the republic. As a result, his dominance was established over the whole of northern Bihar and eastern India, including Vajji and Malla. Ajatashatru protected Rajagriha from the possible attack of the king Pradyota, the ruler of Avanti. In 484 BC, Ajatashatru launched a campaign against the Licchavis and the republics. According to A.L. Basham, Gautama Buddha supported Licchavi and the republics in the battle of Licchavi and the republics with Ajatashatru. Dwijendra Narayan Jha thinks that the republican states had to accept defeat because of their inherent weakness. Magadha was founded on a strong foundation due to the conquest of Kosala and Vaishali. According to A.L. Basham, Bimbisara and Ajatashatru followed the same policy in their policy of expanding the Magadha Empire. The establishment of control over the Ganges in the conduct of Magadha's trade was successful and the empire of Magadha expanded further. Although Ajatashatru had respect for Buddhism, he maintained good relations with Mahavira. It is known from the Bharhut inscription that Ajatashatru traveled to this region which is associated with Gautama Buddha. He installed Chaitya in Rajgriha. The first Buddhist council was performed in the palace on the initiative of Ajatashatru. Ajatashatru died in about 462 BC.

The Ruler of the Haryanka Dynasty After Ajatashatru

After Ajatashatru, his son Darasoka and his grandson Udayin ascended the throne of Magadha. According to Jain and Buddhist sources, his son Udayin ascended the throne after Ajatashatru. Udayin built the village of Pataliputra as the town of Pataliputra. During the reign of Udayin, Pataliputra became the capital of Magadha. The location of Gandak, Son and Ganges rivers facilitated communication and trade in Pataliputra. After Udayin's death, there were three rulers:

(a) Anuruddha,
(b) Munda, and
(c) Nagadasaka.

Shaishunaga Dynasty (430-364 B.C.)

Shishunaga established the Shaishunaga dynasty in about 430 BC by assassinating Nagadashaka, the ruler of the Haryanka dynasty. Shishunaga also handed over the capital first to Rajgir and later to Vaishali. Avanti Mahajanapada, including Shishunaga Ujjain, was included in the Magadha Empire. After the Shishunaga dynasty, Kakavarna or Kalashoka shifted the capital of Magadha to Pataliputra. The second Buddhist council was called in Vaishali during the period of Kalashoka or Kakavarna. According to Banabhatta's "*Harshacharita*", it is believed that Nandivardhana ascended the throne of Panchamaka Magadha after Kalashoka. But they were incompetent. Mahapadma Nanda started the Nanda dynasty in Magadha by killing Kalashoka or Kakavarna.

Nanda Dynasty (364-324 B.C.)

Mahapadmananda founded the Nanda dynasty. In the "Mahavamsa-tika", Mahapadmananda was called 'Ugrasena'. He was known to Greek writers as 'Agrammes'. According to the Puranas, Mahapadmananda was of low caste or Shudra lineage. But Mahapadmananda had an outstanding achievement in making Magadha strong. According to the Puranas, Mahapadmananda is referred to as 'Sarvakshatrandaka' and 'Ekrat'. Apart from this, he established Magadha on a strong foundation by uprooting the Kshstriya dynasties like Panchala, Kasi, Ikshvaku, Haihaya, Ashmaka, Kalinga, Kuru, Maithal etc. According to Dr. Hemchandra Roychowdhury, Mahapadmananda was the founder of the first empire of ancient India. According to Dr. Kallidaikurichi Aiyah Nilkanta Shastri, Mahapadmananda was of low descent but by merit he was the best king of the time.

Dhanananda

In the later period of Mahapadma Nanda, his eight children ascended the throne one after the other. Although none of them could firmly establish the foundation of the Nanda Empire. Then the ninth Nanda or Dhanananda sits on the throne. He was known as 'Augrasainya'. He was also called 'Ugrasena'. The most important event in the reign of Dhanananda was the arrival of the Greek invader Alexander in India in 327 BC. The Greeks also called Dhanananda 'Agrammes' or 'Xandrames' or 'Gendrames'. According to the Greeks, the capital of Agrammes was Pataliputra. The amount of wealth was much higher during the period of Dhanananda. With the help of this wealth, Dhanananda built a strong army. According to Greek mythology, Dhanananda had 200,000 infantry, 20,000 cavalry, 3,000 war elephants, and 2,000 chariots. Chanakya or Vishnugupta, a diplomat and a resident of Takshashila, was appointed as Dhanananda's minister. He was humiliated by Dhanananda and with the help of Chanakya, Chandragupta Maurya killed Dhanananda and established the Maurya dynasty in 324 BC.

Rise of the Magadha Empire: Reason

Dr. Ramesh Chandra Majumdar mentions the prosperity of Magadha in the context of the rise of the Magadha Empire. This rise marked the beginning of a new empire politically. There were various reasons for the rise of the Magadha Empire. Dr. Hemchandra Roychowdhury magnified the achievements of the rulers of the Magadha Empire for its rise.

Strong Ruler

Many historians believe that efficient rulers and diplomatic personalities were one of the key factors in the rise of the Magadha Empire. Behind the rise of this empire were skilled leaders like Bimbisara and Ajatashatru of the Haryanka dynasty. With the presence of powerful rulers like Mahapadmananda and Dhanananda of the Nanda dynasty, Magadha easily established itself as a powerful Mahajanapada. Raja Prasenjit or King Pasenadi in Kosala, Pradyota in Avanti, Udayin in Vatsa Mahajanapada were quite efficient rulers. But those empires could not become as strong as Magadha because they did not have a suitable legacy. Hemchandra Roychowdhury, in his book "Political History of Ancient India", rightly remarked that Magadha played the same role in the politics of ancient India as the pre-Norman Wessex in England and Hohenzollern in Germany for strong leadership like Bimbisara and Nanda. The Minister of the Ajatashatru, Bossaskar, was compared to Machiavelli. Diplomatically unique, Kautilya Chandragupta was Maurya's minister.

Geographical Location

The geographical location of Magadha helped in the rise of Magadha. Initially, the capital of Magadha, Rajgir, was surrounded by five mountains and was naturally protected. In the later period, the capital of Magadha, Pataliputra, was surrounded by the Ganges, Son and Gandak rivers, and Magadha was militarily secure. No other Mahajanapada in the kingdom of Magadha had such an advantageous geographical position.

Expansion of Shipping

Historian Romila Thapar emphasized the importance of shipping behind the rise of the Magadha Empire. A large part of the river Ganges flowed within Magadha. As a result, goods were exchanged by water from eastern India to Varanasi. After capturing 'Anga', Magadha also took over the port of 'Champa'. With the help of the port of Champa, trade was conducted with South India and Southeast Asia. As a result of defeating the Licchavi, Magadha conquered the two shores of Vaishali and Ganges. Thus, Magadha maintained its dominance in the field of shipping. Apart from this, Magadha also prospered in the field of land trade. Magadha dominated the land trade from northeastern India to southern Orissa.

Use of Iron

The use of iron was one of the reasons behind the rise of the Magadha Empire. Magadha was rich in iron resources. There was an iron mine on the Barabar hill near the palace of Gaya and Rajagriha under Magadha. During this time iron was widely used in everyday work and in the manufacture of weapons. The use of iron forks and iron plows greatly improved agriculture. Magadha was rich not only in iron but also in copper. Iron and copper were found in Dhalbhum and

Singbhum areas. Kautilya mentioned in his 'Arthashastra' that the treasury was dependent on mining. With the help of iron, Magadha was enriched militarily and with the help of iron axes and other iron tools, the forests were cleared and agriculture was arranged.

Population

The population of Magadha helped in the rise of the Magadha Empire. In agriculture, huge populations were needed to keep iron and copper mines in operation. Magadha did not lack it. Magadha's prosperity increased due to its large population. In the Ganges-Jamuna Doab region, a large part of the population focused on agriculture by clearing forests. A large part of the population was involved in trade. Magadha also became militarily strong due to its large population. During Alexander's reign, Dhanananda's military presence was so large that it was a matter of concern for a victorious hero like Alexander. Dhanananda had an army of 20,000 cavalry and 200,000 infantry.

Expansion of Aryan-Non-Aryan Culture

The location of Magadha in the central Gangetic valley led to the spread of urban Aryan culture in the culture of Magadha and non-Aryan culture in the lower Gangetic region. To the north-west of the Magadha Empire was the centre of Aryan culture and to the north-east was the centre of non-Aryan culture. In this way it was possible to spread Aryan and non-Aryan culture in Magadha. Since Aryan culture entered Magadha much later, there was no orthodoxy of Brahmanical religion. Non-Aryan culture was prevalent in the lower Gangetic valley. The protesting religious movements of Mahavira and Gautama Buddha put Magadha on a stronger footing.

Strong Monarchy and Political Ideology

Dwijendra Narayan Jha considers the establishment of a strong monarchy in Magadha to be one of the reasons for the rise of the Magadha Empire. At the end of the Vedic period, organizations like sabha and samiti lost their importance. Instead, upper caste organizations supported the monarchy. The Dharmashastras called for the unification of divided India through the terms 'Ekrat', 'Rajchakravarti', 'Virat' etc. The strong monarchy of Magadha fully supported the call for a united India. The political ideology of Magadha helped in the rise of Magadha. Magadha entered politics more than other Mahajanapadas and succeeded in turning the fragmented and scattered Magadha Empire into a large empire.

6 EXPEDITIONS OF PERSIANS AND MACEDONIANS

In his book "Foreign Influence on Ancient India", Krishnachandra Sagar states that most of the foreign invasions in India came from the north-west. The invasion of the Persians was no exception to this rule. Cyrus established the Achaemenid Empire. This empire was formed in Persia. Cyrus invaded parts of eastern Iran in 558-530 BC. He also carried out some expeditions in the border areas of India during this period. Cyrus conquered the region of Gandhara. During the reign of Darius-I (522-486 BC), the Persians invaded India. Darius invaded India and occupied the north-western frontier provinces of India. He then occupied the Indus and Punjab territories in 516 BC. The region was occupied by the Persians until the time of Alexander's expedition to India. Understandably, such expeditions by the Persians were of special importance inside India. The military expedition that took place in India during the time of the Darius-I was led by the skilled commander Skylax. He sailed from the Indian Ocean to the Persian Gulf. Under the leadership of Skylax, Darius-I dominated parts of Gandhara and the Punjab. Gandhara was the most populous, most fertile region of the Achaemenid Empire. According to Herodotus, the region was ruled by a prince named Kshatrap. Gold powder and 360 talent revenue could be obtained from this region. During the reign of Darius-I, Persian domination was established not only in Gandhara but also in the Indus region. According to the Greek scholar Herodotus, Darius-I was the first to send a naval expedition to conquer the Indus basin in 517 BC. The inscription 'Naksh-e-Rostam' shows that the people of Gandhara region were subjects under the Persians. Herodotus first mentions the region of Gandhara occupied by Darius as an important province of his empire. Takshashila, the capital of Gandhara, was also quite prosperous at that time. Indians were also included in the Persian army.

End of Persian Domination in India

After the death of Darius-I, Xerxes was elected chief of the Persians. Soon after being elected, he became embroiled in a conflict with Greece. As a result, he could not concentrate on India at all. It is noteworthy though that he recruited many Indians into his army during war between the Greeks and the Persians. Coming to power after Darius-I, Xerxes was able to maintain the influence of the Persians in India, but he was no longer able to expand his empire. After losing the war with Greece, the Persian Empire fell in India. Nevertheless, the Achaemenid Empire ruled India until 330 BC. It was during this period that Darius-III received Indian help against the army of Alexander. Alexander's expedition to India resulted in the fall of the Persian Empire in India.

The Result of the Persian Campaign

The relations of the Persians with India lasted for about 200 years. During this time the regions under the Persians underwent special economic prosperity. Vincent Smith told us this information in his book. As a result of the Persian invasion and campaign, the administrative, commercial, cultural and political aspects of this country changed. The Persian expedition to India was confined to certain areas of northwestern India. As a result, the Persian campaign had no direct effect on the whole of India. The Persian campaign had no effect on Indian politics or administration. There is no account of the Persian invasion in the ancient literature or mythology of India. During the Persian invasion, the Indian rulers focused on the Magadha Empire. As a result, the Persian expedition did not have much significance as the Indian rulers focused on dominating Magadha. But as a result of the Persian campaign, the influence of the Persians was noticeable in the economy, art, architecture, sculpture and culture of India.

Political and Administrative Influence

The Persian expeditions to India were limited to certain areas of north-western India. As a result, the Persians did not have any special political influence in the whole of India. Thus, the weakness of the Indian military in this region was revealed. This weakness lasted until Alexander's expedition to India. In the case of administrative system, the Persians introduced the system of 'Kshatrap'. This system later affected the Sakas and the Kushans as well. Following the traditional administrative system of the Persians, the Indians also set out to establish a larger empire. The Indians had learned from the Persian expedition that it was necessary to form a skilled and strong army to defend the country from the onslaught of foreign powers. As there were conflicts among the Indian rulers, rivalries and conflicts among the smaller kingdoms, the Indians came together and realized how to resist foreign aggression. Vincent Smith thinks that the Mauryan emperors also adopted imperialist policies under the influence of the Persians.

Relations between India and The Persians

After the Persians invaded India, naturally the Persians formed a relationship with India. Xerxes, the next emperor of Darius-I, included many Indians in his army. Many archers joined the Persian army. The Persians took many invaluable resources from India to Persia. Xerxes used the Indian army on the battlefield against the Greeks. As a result of the Persian expedition, Indian scholars went to Persia. As a result, good relations were established between the two countries.

Cultural Influences

Cultural contacts were established between India and the Persians. The wooden palace of Pataliputra of the Mauryan emperor Chandragupta Maurya was built in imitation of the 'Persepolis' palace in Persia. The Mauryas celebrated many festivals in imitation of the Persians. After the destruction of the city Persepolis by Alexander, many Persian architects and sculptors migrated to India. This led to the use of Indo-Persian style in Indian architecture. The use of Indo-Persian style can be seen in the pillars of Asoka. The Persians spread the use of *Aramaic* script. The *Aramaic* script was found during the time of Asoka. According to *Mortimer* Wheeler, Asoka's pillars were decorated with lion statues, lotuses, and engraved inscriptions under the influence of Persian sculpture. In Asoka's inscription, the words 'Vipi', 'Nipistha' etc. were taken from the Persians. The use of Kharoshthi script can be seen in the Gandhara region. This script was also contributed by the Persians.

Commercial Impact

Vincent Arthur Smith commented that 360 gold coins were collected annually from the Gandhara region as revenue. Trade relations between India and the Persians also developed as a result of good communication between them. In Persia there was a demand for various products made of Indian teak wood and ivory. Lots of Persian coins were found in the north-western frontier region. Thus, it is inferred that there were commercial transactions between Persia and India. Due to the influence of the Persians, the use of iron was found in large numbers in India after the sixth century BC. The Persians showed skill in making gold and silver coins. Inspired by them, the Indians were also successful in making gold and silver coins.

Alexander's Invasion of India

According to N.G. Hammond's "Sources for Alexander the Great", Alexander was the king of the Argead dynasty, which ruled over the ancient Greek kingdom of Macedon. He was world famous as 'Alexander the Great'. He was hailed as an invincible warrior and one of the most successful generals in history by Bill Yenne in his famous book, "The Alexander the Great: Lessons from History's Undefeated General". Speaking of himself, Alexander remarked: "I am not afraid of an army of lions led by a sheep; I am afraid of an army of sheep led by a lion". Alexander-III of Macedon was born on July 20/21, 356 BC, in Pella. He conducted military operations in Northeast Africa and West Asia for most of his reign. He tried to establish a large empire from Egypt to northwestern India by 326 BC. Alexander was a very determined person. He had the ambition to reach the end of the world. John Watson McCrindle states in his book "The Invasion of India by Alexander the Great as described by Arrian" that Alexander invaded and invaded Afghanistan, Punjab, Indus, Grodia and Carmenia. Alexander had a strong appearance. It was his personality that set him apart from other kings. Alexander the Great was as strong and powerful as a lion. Alexander is said to have had a lion's skin wrapped around his head. Alexander, a disciple of the Greek philosopher Aristotle, was called the "King of Half the World."

Alexander's Expedition to India: Background

In his book "The Alexander the Great: Lessons from History's Undefeated General", Bill Ianne called Alexander a "great warrior and undefeated general." Alexander's expedition to India was marked by his 'great warrior' appearance. Alexander the Great invaded Persia in 330 BC. After the invasion of the Persian Empire he conquered there and began his expedition to the east of the Persian Empire. At that time the Persian Empire extended as far as the Indus River or the western border of the Indian subcontinent. At that time many states in the north-western region of India were divided. As a result, they did not have the strength to resist external attacks. By 328 BC, Alexander had conquered Persia and Afghanistan. Then Alexander began to think of occupying the land of the more ancient days. After crossing the Hindu Kush Mountains in 327 BC, he moved further east. Advancing to the banks of the Kabul or Kofen rivers, Alexander's army destroyed Puselaotis, or Charsadda, north of the present-day city of Peshawar. Alexander then marched to the Swat Valley to protect the left side of his army. Inevitably, he occupied the Swat region and recognized the various classes of people there as slaves. He also gained the rights of a large number of cattle in the Swat region. Incidentally, Alexander's acquisition of Swat was not easy. The Assyrian tribes there put up strong resistance against Alexander's forces. Assakenoi was the chief of this tribe. This ethnic group was named after him. Asakenus conceded defeat to Alexander's brilliant tactics as the city of Massaga (the capital of Assakenoi) was besieged despite his best efforts. Alexander then captured the cities of Aonas and Nisa. After crossing the Indus, Alexander entered India in 326 BC. He crossed the Hindu Kush Mountain to start marching towards India in 327 BC. Michael Wood mentions in his book. "In the Footsteps of Alexander the Great: A Journey from Greece to Asia" that Alexander's expedition towards Asia was something very adventurous. His expedition to India was also very adventurous.

Alexander's Invasion of India: North-west India

Alexander was one of the most successful warriors in the history of the world. The reason for his success was his invincible attitude—as Richard Stoneman puts it in his book—"*Alexander the Great*". Alexander was the son of Philip II, king of Macedon. He was world famous as a victorious hero. When he invaded India, there was political disunity in the north-western part of India. No individual strong state has yet developed in northwestern India. Politically, this chaotic situation made Alexander's occupation of India much easier. At that time there were seven different states living in the area between Jhelum and Beas (Vipasha) rivers and the whole region was divided into many small kingdoms. The names of these republican and monarchical states can be deduced from the Greek account. Such as:

(A) The Aspasioi tribes lived in the mountainous region north of the Kabul River.
(B) Nicaea or Kikaia State situated between Kabul and Indus rivers.
(C) The Gauris rule on the banks of the river Gauri or Panjikora.
(D) Equestrian or equestrian kingdom in the Swart or Bunar area.
(E) Puraskaravati of present day Peshawar district.
(F) Ursha state of Hazra district.
(G) Takshashila state in present day Rawalpindi district.
(H) Kantha State.
(I) Malava State.
(J) Shudra kingdom.

(K) Soubhutir state on the banks of the river Jhelum.
(L) The kingdom of Gandhara, situated to the east of the Mahajanapada of ancient Gandhara.
(M) The hill state Avisar to the north of Takshashila.
(N) Porus or Poros state between Jhelum and Chenab rivers. These states were political rivals. As a result conflicts continued all the time. Conflict between the king of Takshashila Ambhi and the kingdom of Porus and Abhisar was a daily affair. In the midst of political unrest, these states of northwestern India were not strong enough to resist Alexander's invasion. Conflict weakened them a lot.

Alexander's Invasion of India: Purpose

Alexander wanted to subdue the whole world. As a result, from the very beginning he focused on the expansion of the kingdom. Ramashankar Tripathi in his book "History of Ancient India" commented that his expedition to India was also an attempt to fulfill this aspiration of state expansion. At the same time, in this book, he discusses Alexander's conflict with Porus. After the conquest of Persia, Alexander entered India to expand his empire. His main goal was to conquer the Persian Empire. After the conquest of Persia, Alexander set out on a journey to the eastern frontier of Darius' empire. This is how he reached the north-western border of India. Alexander was very curious in nature. His interest in knowing the world was infinite. He was curious about the extent of the Caspian Sea. For this reason he expressed interest in the India expedition with the aim of reaching eastern part of the Caspian Sea. The information regarding India he got from Herodotus and it encouraged him in his expedition to India. Various accounts of the book of Herodotus mention India's vast wealth. Alexander the Great is believed to have been inspired by the wealth of India as described in the book of Herodotus. That is why he tried to invade India. Alexander's attitude towards conquering new territories and spreading Greek culture in those territories is evident. This is why Alexander invaded India.

Alexander: Entering India

John Ralph discussed the subject of Alexander's heroism in his book, "History of Alexander", edited by Quintus Curtius Rufus. Alexander entered India and faced stiff resistance, but his victory was not without problems. In early 327 BC, Alexander marched on India, conquering Bactria, Bokhara, Sirdaria, and Nikaya. He set up camp in the kingdom of Nikaya. From Nikaya he sent messengers to the king of Takshashila. He told the envoy that the Indian king should surrender to him without a fight. Before Alexander reached Takshashila, Ambhi sent envoys to Alexander. He said through an envoy that if Alexander refrained from attacking Takshashila, he would cooperate with Alexander in every possible way. Ambhi sent 65 elephants, about 10,000 sheep and about 3,000 bulls as gifts to Alexander. Apart from Ambhi, Alexander also got help from kings like Sanjay, Ashwajit, Kofius, Shashigupta. With the help of these rulers, Alexander entered India with about 30,000 troops.

Alexander's Expedition to India: Resistance

Vincent Arthur Smith commented on Alexander's expedition to India that no other event in Indian history was as astonishing to European readers as Alexander the Great's Macedonian expedition to India in 326 BC. However, it is also true that Alexander's conquest of India was not an easy one. He too had to face a lot of resistance. Initially, Alexander's conquest was resisted by many small kingdoms and their kings. The people of some republicans also resisted Alexander's invasion. King Ashtak of Pushkaravati (Peukelaotis) confronted Alexander with his little strength. He died after 30 days of fighting. The Ashwan (Aspasioi) and Assakenoi (Asvakayana) then tried to resist Alexander's expedition. He also had to work hard and fight to conquer the two protected cities of Andak and Mahikavai (Mahim). But Alexander the Great overcame this resistance by conquering the city of Nisa, the city between the Indus and Pushkaravati, and the fort of the hills, and entered India in 326 BC.

The Conflict between Alexander and Porus

During Alexander's expedition to India, the rulers of Takshashila and its environs obeyed Alexander. But the patriotism of king Porus in the region between Jhelum and Chandrabhaga was the matter of best repute. Although the neighbouring kingdoms were loyal to Alexander, Porus maintained his determination of not surrendering to Alexander. Alexander crossed the Indus with his army in 326 BC. Arrangements were made to build a boat bridge near the Attock (Ampbellpur) region. To the east of the Persian frontier was the Indus River. Alexander then set out for Takshashila. Takshashila was the prosperous capital of King Ambhi. He helped Alexander's expedition without any resistance. Although Ambhi helped Alexander in his motive of conquering many states of India, but Porus did not go for an agreement with Alexander. Alexander organized a meeting at Takshashila. The surrendering king and Porus were also invited to the meeting. Porus reluctantly declined the invitation and informed Alexander's envoy that he could not leave any part of his kingdom without a fight. In the end, Alexander prepared for war to capture the kingdom of Porus. On both sides of the Jhelum River, Porus and Alexander's army began preparations for battle. Alexander was not interested in a war with Porus. That is why in the darkness of the night, Alexander and his army advanced 17 miles along the Jhelum river. Early in the next morning, Alexander crossed the Jhelum River and attacked Porus. Porus was not at all prepared of this sudden attack. He lost his life on the battlefield. The state of Porus, Hydaspes, was situated between the rivers Jhelum and Chandrabhaga. As the kingdom of Hydaspes was situated between the Jhelum and Chandrabhaga rivers, the king thought it was very safe and secure. But Porus's army was defeated by Alexander's powerful army.

The Battle of Hydaspes between Alexander and Porus

Vincent Arthur Smith commented on the Battle of Hydaspes between Alexander and Porus, saying that Alexander's victory in the Battle of Hydaspes between Alexander and Porus further enhanced Alexander's reputation and prestige. Alexander also made a treaty with Porus. Alexander with his army crossed the Jhelum River and was interrupted by flooding. Alexander had cavalry. But seeing the elephants lined up in Porus, Alexander changed his tactics. After waiting for a few weeks on the banks of the Jhelum River, he instructed the army to cross the river through a narrow bend in the Jhelum River. He fought against Alexander with a strong and efficient army. Alexander the Great's vast army landed at the battle of Hydaspes or Jhelum with the Porus army. According to Vincent Arthur Smith, the battle of Hydaspes or Jhelum took place in the area between Shirwal and Pakhran. In the Porus army there were (a) infantry, (b) chariots, (c) cavalry, and (d) elephants. Porus also had to deal with natural disasters at the Battle of Hydaspes. But the wheel of the chariot of Porus became helpless to settle in the mud. Alexander's army attacked Porus's army and Porus was wounded in the battle of Hydaspes. But the heroism of Porus was significant. Porus was 6 feet tall and had injuries in about 9 places on his body. Fascinated by Porus's courage and heroism, the prisoner Porus was greeted by Alexander. When Porus was brought before Alexander, Alexander wanted to know what Porus expected from him. In reply, Porus said that one king expects another king to behave like a king. Alexander was impressed by Porus's heroism and returned Porus to his kingdom. In addition, Porus donated 15 more republics to the east of his kingdom. A treaty was signed between Porus and Alexander. According to Vincent Arthur Smith, the main reason for Alexander's victory in the battle of Hydaspes was the skillful leadership of Alexander, the greatest general in the history of the world. In his book "Historical Dictionary of Greek Warfare", written by J. Oronoff and Ispens, he states that Porus or Porusshottam ruled as a feudal kingdom under Alexander after his defeat on the banks of the Vetesta or Jhelum River in 326 BC.

Alexander's Expeditions to India and Elsewhere

John Ralph discusses the success of Alexander's expeditions in his book, "The History of Alexander", edited by Quintus Curtius Rufus. During the expedition to India, Alexander defeated Porus and advanced further east. In order to be militarily strong, he was able to destroy two powerful tribes, namely—

(a) Glausai and
(b) Slaconicoi, even in the face of natural disasters.

Not only these two tribes, but Alexander's army also destroyed the 'Khudrakas' and the 'Bipasha' and the 'Kathoth' tribes by crossing the Chandrabhaga River. His army then crossed the Beas (Vipasa) River and advanced further east. But tired, they did not agree to any further expedition to the east. Presumably, Alexander was hesitant to head east towards Bihar on hearing of the infinite heroism of the kingdom of Magadha. Although in the area east of the Beas (Vipasa) River he left his signature of world conquest. He ordered to build 12 pillars in this area and engrave them in inscriptions. These pillars were later obliterated due to the diversion of the Beas (Vipasa) River. As a result of the conflict within his own army, Alexander decided to return to the path he had taken.

Alexander's Expedition to India: Results

Krishnachandra Sagar in his book "Foreign Influence in Ancient India" discusses the impact or results of Alexander's expedition to India. In this text, Krishnachandra Sagar states that the Greeks gained a lot of knowledge about India as a result of Alexander's expedition. Many new teachings were adopted by the Greeks from India. Alexander's invasion of India gave rise to much clearer ideas about Indian philosophy and religion. In this context, Vincent Arthur Smith said that as a result of this campaign, the communication system with India has improved a lot.

Improvement of the Communication System

According to Vincent Arthur Smith, Alexander's expedition to India improved the communication between India and abroad. As a result, 3 land routes and 1 waterway were discovered between India and abroad. These waterways and land routes made it easier to communicate between different countries in India and abroad. Radhakumud Mukherjee said that the only lasting effect of Alexander's expedition to India was the improvement of communication between India and Greece.

Establishment of Greek Colonies

Alexander invaded India from the north-west. As a result, several Greek colonies were formed in the border areas of northern India. Of these, four Greek colonies were notable.

(a) Nicaea or Nikaia in the area where the war with Porus took place.
(b) Alexandria at the confluence of the Indus and Chandrabhaga rivers.
(c) Sogdian Alexandria at the confluence of the rivers of the Punjab.
(d) Bucephala (Bucephalia) in the area where Alexander crossed the Jhelum river.

In these colonies Alexander left many Greeks to maintain Europe's connection with India. However, many Greeks did not want to leave Greece. As a result, the colonies did not last long.

Spread of European Knowledge

Vincent Arthur Smith remarked that Alexander's expedition had no direct effect on India. Although the expedition was indirect, it was able to exert some influence over the country. Alexander's army returned to the country and spread their experience of India to other parts of Europe. As a result, knowledge about the geography and different regions of India spread in Europe. Alexander was a curious man. His passion for learning about different countries was strong. As a result, his expedition to India also enriched his experience. It was on the basis of this experience that Alexander informed Nyarkas, the chief of his navy, that the Indus Valley could be reached from the Indus Basin to the Persian Gulf via the Indian Ocean. This increased the geographical knowledge of the Europeans about the East and India.

Introduction of the Precise Governance

Alexander divided his territory into seven parts. Five of them were

Indian territories; the other two were border areas. In all of these regions, Alexander introduced precise regimes. The two frontier regions under Alexander formed the states between the Hindu Kush Mountains and the Indus River. One ruler was appointed in each of the five provinces of the Indian Territory.

(a) A Greek military leader was appointed governor of the Indus Valley Province.
(b) The Greek leader Philip was appointed governor of the province south of Kabul, in the middle of the Chandrabhaga River.
(c) King Ambhi of Takshashila was appointed governor of the province comprising the region between Jhelum and the Indus.
(d) Alexander's father-in-law, Oksartsek, was appointed governor of the territory north of Kabul, Afghanistan.
(e) The man was appointed governor of the province comprising the region between the rivers Jhelum and Beas (Vipasa).

Alexander left some Greek troops for this security. The Greek provinces were not permanent. After Alexander's death, Greek rulers moved westward from the region. As a result, the native rulers later formed independent states in their territories.

Progress in Trade

Before Alexander's expedition, Europe had no land or sea communication with the Indian subcontinent. This journey became easier after Alexander's expedition. Three land routes from Persia and Afghanistan to India were discovered. These three routes are:

(a) Kabul,
(b) Moola Pass in Balochistan, and
(c) Gedrosia.

It was through these three routes that the trade relations of the Eastern countries with Europe were formed. Even commercial progress was noticed.

Cultural Outcomes

Alexander's invasion of India led to the development of cultural exchanges between East and West. According to Vincent Arthur Smith, the bridge between East and West has a Hellenistic influence on Indian art. Greek influences can be seen in the sculptures of Gandhara region. Without the Greek Hellenistic influence, the pattern of Gandhara art found in Takshashila, Pakistan, would never have been possible. According to Hermes Gomez, Gandhara's art originated from a mixture of Buddhist and Greek art. The statues found in the region were made in the Hellenistic-Syrian style. Greek influence can also be seen in Indian culture. This influence is particularly noticeable in Indian drama and literature. The Indians imitated the Greek currency. The Indian word 'dam' comes from the Greek word 'drachma'. In contrast, the influence of Indian sculpture and art can be seen in the making of statues and coins of Greek and Roman deities. Alexander's Greek colonization of the north-western frontier had a profound effect on Indian culture, and Indian influence was also seen in Greek culture.

Influence in the Religious Field

According to Vincent Arthur Smith, the influence of paganism in Buddhism's 'Mahayana' was influenced by Greek paganism. The influence of Buddhism was also found in the Gnostic Christian community. Indian sculpture and art were introduced in the method of making idols of Greek deities. 'Mahayana' Buddhism also influenced the Greeks. The Greeks learned religion and philosophy from Buddhists and Vaisnavas. The two Greek scholars were—

(a) Minander and
(b) Heliodorus.

Buddhist influence was also seen in Christianity. The goods of the Indian subcontinent reached different parts of Europe through the Caspian and Black Seas. Not only in Europe, had India developed trade relations with various Central Asian countries for new routes.

Results of Alexander's Expedition to India: Evaluation

Historian Vincent Arthur Smith says that Alexander's expedition to India made it possible to establish a link between the West and the East, although historians have expressed the complete opposite view of Havel. According to Havel, since the Persians had come to the north-western frontier of the country before Alexander, Alexander's expedition to India could not find a new path. Paul Mason comments—The importance of Alexander's expedition was quite damaging. According to Vincent Arthur Smith, Alexander's expedition to India did not directly affect the people of India. However, this expedition created a link between India and Greece. Cultural and commercial exchanges were also possible. According to the historian Niyese, the administrative system of the later period of India was based on the administrative system introduced by Alexander.

BUDDHISM AND JAINISM

7

K.T.S. Sarao and J. Free. D Long discuss the causes and context of the rise of Buddhism and Jainism in their book "Buddhism and Jainism". In this text they show why the people of that time adopted Buddhism and Jainism. The Vedic religion of India had various complexities and sacrifices. Such errors in the Vedic religion set the stage for the protest movement. Buddhism and Jainism were born in the context of this protest. Buddhism and Jainism emerged as protest religions in the sixth century BC. Buddhism spread not only in India but in different parts of the world. In his book "The Age of Iron and The Religious Revolution", Krishnamohan Srimali discusses the protest movement against the Vedic religion and raises the issue of about 363 religious ideologies with the help of Buddhist and Jain scriptures. Ajit kesh Kamblin's Lokayat Dharma and Makkhali Gosala's Ajivika Dharma were important in the protest movement.

Buddhism-Jainism: The Cause of the Defendant Religion Movement

We have already seen that Buddhism and Jainism were born out of opposition to the Vedic religion. There were various reasons behind the rise of these two religions. Pranashankar Someshwar Joshi discusses Buddhism and Jainism in the context of the defendant religion movement in his book "Ancient Indian History: Civilization and Culture".

Economic and Social Changes

Xavier Pinto and E.G. Maitpal analyzed in their book entitled

"Glimpses of History" the various reasons behind the rise of Buddhism and Jainism as a protest movement. They say that the predominance of the priestly class in the Vedic religion gave birth to disgust among the common people. From there these two religions came up in protest. Apart from this, the worship system of Vedic religion was quite complicated. Yajnas, animal sacrifices, etc. were always there. The popularity and spread of Buddhism and Jainism was because of their relatively easy mode of worship. Batindranath Mukherjee, in his book "Genesis of Buddhism: Its Social Content", opined that economic and social changes were observed in the society in the sixth century BC. As a result, economic and social inequality became very wide. People then began to focus on simple living. The emergence of the city in society, the increase in the number of artisan classes, the expansion of industrial trade brought about changes in the economic and social spheres which influenced the religious ideology. In this context, the rise of Buddhism and Jainism was facilitated.

Predominance of Kshatriyas

According to historian Romila Thapar, social inequality culminated in the Vedic period. On the one hand, there was a class of special people who were entitled to special privileges. On the other hand, there were poor people, who were in need. As a result, the issue of social equality

Parshvanatha and his Yaksha

Gautama Buddha

promoted by Buddhism touched the masses at that time. However, the dominance of the Kshatriya class in the society helped in the rise of Buddhism and Jainism. At that time there was a situation of conflict between Brahmins and Kshatriyas. The Kshatriyas had considerable respect and dignity in the society as a warrior class. But the Vedic

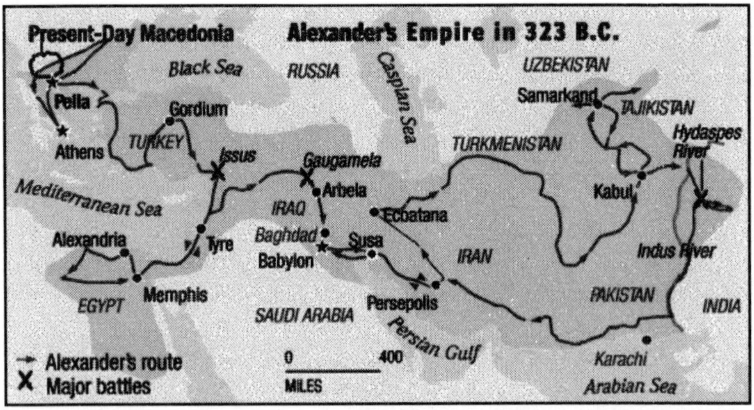

Alexander's Empire in 323 BC

religion acknowledged the superiority of the Brahmins which the Kshatriyas could not accept. The Kshatriyas were not willing to accept the domination of the Brahmins at all. As a result, many historians believe that the Kshatriyas helped in the rise of Buddhism and Jainism in order to reduce the influence of the Brahmins. Mahavira and Gautama Buddha were Kshatriyas by birth. At that time, the status of Kshatriyas in the society increased due to the continuous war. It was in this context that Buddhism and Jainism emerged. Gautama Buddha preached that it is possible to attain Brahmanism not by birth, but by action. By denying the exclusive authority of the Brahmins, he gave place to the Kshatriyas over the Brahmins.

Attitude Against Yajna and Animal Killing

According to Xavier Pinto and E.J. Maipal, animal slaughter was practiced in the Vedic period. Sacrifice and animal slaughter were one of the aspects of religious rites in the Vedic age. This had a huge impact on the agricultural system. Due to this, ordinary people also faced extreme economic problems. Vedic literature testifies that in spite of the great need for cattle in agriculture, 600 bulls were often sacrificed. Naturally, the peasants and the general public joined the anti-animal slaughter initiative. Buddhist texts say that cow-killing needs to stop in order to increase agricultural resources. Animal slaughter has been opposed in Buddhism and Jainism. The policy of non-violence was welcomed there. As a result, Buddhism and Jainism naturally emerged.

The Rise of the Merchant Class

The rise of the merchant class in the sixth century BC also signaled great changes in the social and economic spheres. This merchant community can be mentioned as the primary patron of Buddhism and Jainism. The 'Shresthi' and 'Sahapati' are found in this merchant class. The merchant groups that were wealthy were known in the city as the 'Shresthi', and in the countryside as the 'Sahapati'. Although this group of merchants was wealthy, they were deprived of their proper status due to caste. However, the Shresthis were active in overcoming the restrictions of the Brahmins to be established in the society. Buddhism and Jainism gave them this opportunity. The urban mentality of the city was much more acceptable than the rural mentality of the Vedic age. Preachers of Buddhism and Jainism played a special role in this regard. The merchant community had a close relationship with Gautama Buddha.

Opposition to Brahmanical Doctrine

Dr. Bratindranath Mukherjee said that Vedic rituals and sacrifices were very expensive. It was a little difficult for ordinary people to observe these rituals. In contrast, the practices of Buddhism and Jainism were not expensive. As a result, the common people were easily drawn to these two religions. It is pertinent to note that Buddhism and Jainism originated by opposing Brahmanical religion. Since Buddhism and Jainism were primarily protestant in nature, casteism did not find a place in these two religions. Besides, there were no atrocities like animal sacrifice. These two religions had no faith in Yajna. These two religions believed that Yajna could not liberate people at all. Honest deeds, honest behaviour, meditation and devotion are required for the liberation of a person. It is understood that Buddhism and Jainism emerged as new religions by opposing Brahmanical doctrine and denying the superiority of Brahmins.

Revolutionary Changes in Agricultural Use

Historian Ramsharan Sharma considers the use of iron in agriculture in the sixth century BC to be an unprecedented change in the agricultural system. Damodar Dharmananda Kosambi thinks that axes and sickles made of iron were used in the sixth century BC. Agriculture was prepared by clearing forests in the central Gangetic valley. At this time iron plow was also used. The result was a revolutionary change in the agricultural system. The use of plows made of iron resulted in increased production in agriculture. Clearing forests using iron axes, axes, etc. increased the amount of agricultural land. This revolutionary change in the agricultural system was contrary to the Vedic school. As a result, the rise of Buddhism and Jainism was easy at this time. Damodar Dharmananda Kosambi and Ramsharan Sharma think that the field of second urbanization was also prepared at that time. According to Dr. Bratindranath Mukherjee, this kind of failure was caused by social and economic inequalities throughout society in the sixth century BC. Buddhism and Jainism guided an acceptable way of life by protecting everyone from that failure. It was under such circumstances that Buddhism and Jainism originated.

Dominance of Vaishya Class and Equality of Women

In the Vedic age Vaishyas or the merchant class were considered as the most neglected class. Due to the dominance of Brahmins at that time their place in the society was quite neglected. The Vaishyas were able to improve themselves in a very short period of time as a result of the gradual improvement of the agricultural system. As a result of becoming rich quickly, the Brahmins also had to rely on the Vaishyas. Naturally financially viable Vaishyas were no longer willing to accept the influence of the Brahmins. Buddhism preached by Gautama Buddha again did not follow this caste system. As a result, Buddhism was sympathetic to the Vaishyas. Naturally the Vaishyas also in return provided financial support for the spread of this new religion. Towards the end of the Vedic age, the position of women gradually became deplorable.

Buddhism: Gautama Buddha

Gautama Buddha was the father and preacher of Buddhism. He was a man of strong personality, although his life was simple. There was no excess of formality or pomp in the religion he preached. As a result, very quickly, Buddhism was able to respond to a large section of the population. Vishvapani Bomfield has portrayed the simple life of Gautama Buddha in his book "Gautama Buddha". An important book to know the biography and theology of Gautama Buddha is "Lalitvistarasutra". Apart from this, the Sinhalese history of the 'Deepavamsha' and the 'Mahavamsha' is noteworthy. The advices and teachings of Gautama Buddha are known from the 'Tripitaka'. According to A.L. Basham, the details left by Buddhist monks about Gautama Buddha are one of the elements of knowledge about Gautama Buddha. Rohini Chowdhury praised Gautama Buddha and said that Buddhism had spread to Tibet, Sri Lanka, South-east Asia, Korea, Japan, China and Central Asia besides India.

Gautama Buddha: Biography

In her book "Gautama Buddha: The Lord of Wisdom", Rohini Chowdhury states that there are differences of opinion about the year of birth of Gautama Buddha. He was probably born in 563 BC. According to historian Geoffrey Samuel, Gautama Buddha was born into a Kshatriya dynasty. He was born in Lumbini Udyan in the city of Kapilavastu in the Terai region of Nepal. His father's name was Suddhodana and his mother was Maya Devi. In the text "Indian Buddhism" K. Warder says that Gautama Buddha's other name is Siddhartha. According to the name of the tribe, he is called Gautama. He was the elected head of the Shakya Republic. Narada commented in his book "A Manual of Buddhism" that eight Brahmins named Siddhartha, the son of Suddhodana, the one who attained Siddhi. After the death of his mother, he was brought up by his mother-in-law Gautami. Gautama Buddha's father Suddhodana was the head of the 'Shakya' Kshatriya group. Gautama Buddha is therefore also called 'Shakyasingha'. Narada said that a saint named Asit saw the newborn Siddhartha and predicted that this child would later become a Raj Chakraborty or Siddha Sadhak. At the age of 18, Gautama Buddha married Yashodhara. He is the father of a son named Rahul. According to Buddhist scriptures, Gautama Buddha's father arranged all the luxuries for his son. Yet Gautama Buddha realized that material wealth was not the goal of his life. The defendant religion movement that developed in the sixth century BC emphasized the importance of women's equality. Gautama Buddha initiated ganika (i.e. prostitute) Amrapali. Protesting movements for women's equality gained more and more popularity.

Exodus

Edward Trunge translated Buddhist texts. From him one can know about Gautama Buddha's "Mahabhinishkramana". When Gautama Buddha came out of the palace at the age of 29, he saw (a) an old man, (b) a sick man, (c) a dead man, and (d) a monk. Siddhartha questioned head charioteer Channa in this regard. Channa told him that every man would one day fall ill and die. He is called a monk who has given up his domestic life for the misery of man. Siddhartha conquers Tritapas (The three forces of destiny) i.e. (a) old age or decay, (b) malady and (c) death. He realized that this was the way to his salvation. At the age of 29, he left the majestic splendor of Suddhodana, his wife Yashodhara and son Rahul and left home with his beloved horse Kanthaka and head charioteer Channa. After saying goodbye to Kanthaka and Channa, he left for the palace. His main goal was to attain Bodhi or absolute knowledge. According to Buddhist scriptures, his departure was known as Mahabhinishkramana.

Realization/Attainment of Bodhi

In his book "Early Buddhism and the Bhagavad Gita", K.N. Upadhyaya says that after leaving home, Siddhartha studied yoga and scriptures with a monk named Alara Kalama. But he did not like the initiation of Alara Kalama on the question of getting rid of Tritap. He then became a disciple of Uddaka Ramputta. But not getting proper answer to his question, he went to a place called Urubilb in Buddhagaya. He then came in contact with five ascetics and inflicted immense suffering on the body, believing that he would be liberated. After 6 years of rigorous austerities, his body turned into a weak skeleton. When he was about to die, he realizes that it is not possible to attain enlightenment by doing hard austerities to the body. He thinks that enlightenment is possible by finding a middle way between extravagant luxurious living and rigorous austerities. He received Paramanna from a daughter named Sujata. He meditated under an ashwattha sacred fig tree in a village called Uruvela on the banks of the Nairanjana River near Gaya. In his book "Introduction to Buddhism: An Exploration of the Buddhist Way of Life", Kelasak Nayatamo says that while meditating under this tree, he vows that he will not leave until he finds the truth. After meditating for 49 days, he attains 'Bodhi' or optimum knowledge or Buddhism. From this time he became Gautama Buddha or Buddha. He found the way out from the clutch of Tritap. As a result, he knew the way to save from rebirth. He attained Nirvana. He was called the chief man of attaining Nirvana in the informative or desired way. As he attained Nirvana under the ashwattha tree, it is known as Bodhi tree and the village of Uruvela is known as 'Bodh Gaya'. It was during this time that he gained insight into human life and its causes and ways to alleviate grief which is known as 'Aryasatyas' (Four noble truths). According to him, it is possible to attain liberation or nirvana by gaining knowledge of this truth.

Buddhism: Arya Satya

Damodar Dharmananda Kosambi in his book mentions 'Arya Satyas' while explaining Buddhism. Everyone in this world, rich or poor or powerful, suffers. Everyone's life is sad. And everyone has to try to get rid of this grief. The birth of this grief is usually due to three reasons:

(a) decay,
(b) disease, and
(c) death. Buddhism originated from the attempt to remove these three sorrows.

The main goal of Buddhism was to realize the truth and remove the sorrows of human life. 'Arya Satyas' was important in the teachings of Buddhism or in theology.

(a) This world is miserable,
(b) The birth of sorrow is from the desire of the person,
(c) Liberation is possible only if this desire can be removed,
(d) For this liberation one has to follow the 'eightfold path'.

According to Gautama Buddha, the Arya Satya or four noble truths is that—

(a) this world is miserable,
(b) there is a cause of sorrow, addiction to lust is the cause of sorrow,
(c) redemption of sorrow is possible,
(d) there is a way to alleviate sorrow, it requires 'Nirvana'.

There are certain ways to follow Nirvana. This particular path is the 'eightfold path'.

Propagation of Buddhism

After attaining enlightenment, Gautama Buddha was met by two persons named Trapusa and Bahalika. They were the first general disciples of Gautama Buddha. He then explained his new religion with five monks in present-day Sarnath and gave the first teachings. According to the Buddhist tradition, this event is known as 'Dhrma- chakra Pravartana'. Yash, the son of a Shresthi, was the first domestic disciple of Gautama Buddha. The first Buddhist association was formed with Yash, his friends and 50 others. From Sarnath he came to Rajagriha. In Rajagriha, this Upasaka or Upasika accepted his discipleship and joined the Buddhist Sangha. They became known as Sariputta and Maudgalyayana or Mahamaudgalyayana. Gautama Buddha then went to Kapilavastu. His son Rahul took initiation from him. The first ten disciples of Gautama Buddha were:

(i) Sariputra,
(ii) Maudgalyayana,
(iii) Mahakasyapa,
(iv) Subhuti,
(v) Purna Maitrayaniputra,

(vi) Katyayana,
(vii) Aniruddha,
(viii) Upali,
(ix) Rahula, and
(x) Ananda.

Gautama Buddha went to Vaishali city. Amrapali of Vaishali gave him mango-grove and joined the Buddhist Association in her last years. Mahaprajapati, the step mother of Gautama Buddha, joined the Gautami-Buddhist Association. Although Gautam Buddha initially objected, he later allowed women to join the association and allowed women to enter the association as nuns. Gautama Buddha preached in cities like—

(a) Beranjana,
(b) Sankosha, and
(c) Kosambi etc.

Gautama Buddha preached in West and South India.

Gautama Buddha: Mahaparinirvana

According to the "The Mahayana Mahaparinirvana Sutra", Gautama Buddha announced his imminent death at the age of 80. Gautama Buddha traveled to Kushinagar. On his way from Vaishali to Kushinara (Kusavati) or Kushinagar, Gautam Buddha fell ill. According to Arthur Wally, he fell ill after eating pork at the home of a blacksmith named Chunda in Pabagram. According to Oscar von Hindubar, Gautama Buddha did not die from poisoning to eat pork. It was due to his old age. Gautama Buddha attained Mahaparinirvana near Kushinagar in 486 BC, according to the *Dipavamsa* and *Mahavamsa*. According to K.C. Aden, Buddhists in Thailand consider March 11, 543 BC, to be the day of Gautama Buddha's death. Gautama Buddha died under a bodhi tree in Kushinagar in present day Gorakhpur district or he attained Mahaparinirvana. Here Gautama Buddha gave his last advice while lying down before his death. His last words were "All worldly things are destined to be destroyed. Thus fight for your own liberation."

Buddhism

Gautama Buddha used an excellent analogy to explain the essence of Buddhism. He said that just as salt is the only taste of sea water, so the only purpose of Buddhism is to get rid of sorrow. Buddhism is actually a religion of teaching people to get rid of sorrow, so Krishnamohan Srimali commented in his book "The Age of Iron and the Religious Revolution". Now what is the way to get rid of this? According to Buddhism, in order to get rid of misery, people need to focus on proper living and correct thinking. Everyone has to live a simple life and follow the code of ethics. Gautama Buddha thinks that every human being is made up of 5 elements:

(a) body,
(b) feeling,
(c) perception,
(d) mental state, and
(e) awareness.

These elements are the cause of human misery. When these five elements change, people die or a new person is born. There is a need to 'Nirvana' to get rid of sorrow. Gautama Buddha emphasized on four truths for attaining Nirvana. Together these four truths are called 'Arya Satyas' ('Four Noble Truths').

Buddhism: The Attainment of Nirvana

In Buddhism, it is believed that after attaining Nirvana, Tritapa, that is, decay-disease-death, does not occur in the mind. Nirvana is the liberation from Tritapa. According to the Buddhist scripture Arya Pariyasena, 'Nirvana' means—

(a) oblivion,
(b) old age,
(c) cure,
(d) deathless,
(e) incomparable,

(f) authorless,
(g) impurity, and
(h) the ultimate goal of man.

The Majjhima Approach

Gautama Buddha's first religious advice, the introduction of Dharmachakra, is the 'Eightfold Path'. This 'eightfold path' is called 'Middle Path'. The path taken by Gautama Buddha for the attainment of Nirvana was known in Buddhism as the 'Majjhima Pantha' or 'Majjhima Approach'. Because Gautama Buddha said to follow the middle path by rejecting both extreme asceticism and extreme austerities, the path between extravagance and hard austerities was the 'meditative approach'.

Eightfold Path

Damodar Dharmananda Kosambi has explained the eightfold path. The eight paths directed by Gautama Buddha to follow were known as the 'Ashtanga Marga'. These eight ways are:

(a) Right Speech: False speech causes a lot of harm to the society. As a result, everyone should stop using unnecessary sentences and use moderate and honest sentences.
(b) Right mindfulness deeds: Such deeds should be done for the benefit of others. Dishonest and immoral activities create chaos in the society.
(c) Right livelihood: Livelihood should be earned in an honest way. People need to get rid of livelihoods that are harmful to society. Such as: wine and meat business.
(d) Right effort: People should not allow bad thoughts to prevail in their mind. Gautama Buddha advised to give place to innate honest thoughts in people.
(e) Right Aspiration: To be constantly aware of honest thoughts.
(f) Right Action: not to increase wealth or power by harming others. Try to make others happier.
(g) Right Thought: To save mental energy by keeping the human mind restrained and controlled. One must constantly think of protecting himself from the evil power.

(h) Right Concentration: Assimilation with a concentrated mind. He also realized that there is sorrow in the world because of man's uncontrolled desires and greed. Peace requires the cessation of desires. This was called honest vision.

Panchasheel

'Panchsheel' is the observance of five ethics. Gautama Buddha told every person to follow five morals. These five principles are:

(i) No Killing—Respect for Life.
(ii) No Stealing—Respect for other's property.
(iii) No sexual misconduct—Respect for our pure nature.
(iv) No Lying—Respect for honesty.
(v) No intoxicants—Respect for a clear mind. Followers of Buddhism call these five principles or teachings 'Panchsheel'.

Tripitaka: Buddhist Scriptures

The name of the ancient Buddhist religious text is 'Tripitaka'. The role of this book is essential to know the basic ideology of Buddhism. The teachings of the Buddha have been compiled in this 'Tripitaka'. 'Tripitaka' is written in Pali. It is divided into three parts—

(a) *Vinaya Pitaka*: This book contains the rules of how to live in the monastery of Buddhist monks and nuns.
(b) *Sutta Pitaka* or *Sutra Pitaka*: Ethical rules compiled by the Buddha are contained in this book.
(c) *Abhidhamma Pitaka* or *Abhidharma Pitaka*: These are spiritual and philosophical interpretations of Buddhism.

Mahayana Doctrine: Hinayana Doctrine

In Gautama Buddha's doctrine, there are three ways of liberation:

(a) seeking personal liberation,
(b) trying to do well to others, and
(c) trying for the liberation of others without thinking of one's own liberation.

The Hinayanas made the first two attempts and the Mahayana took the last approach. In the Mahayana doctrine, deity is imposed on Gautama Buddha. These followers emphasize Gautama Buddha's devotion to theology and his attainment of Bodhisattva. Mahayana people also believe in idol worship of Gautama Buddha. The Mahayana thought that the canons of *Sutta Pitaka* were the main advice of Gautama Buddha. On the other hand, the Hinayanas were in favour of paying homage to Gautama Buddha. They gave more importance to Abhidharma Pitaka. The Hinayanas believed in atheism. They emphasized monasticism and monasticism.

Buddhism: Influence and Spread

According to Will Durant, Gautama Buddha was one of the first reformers in human society to speak of religion in a simple way. The influence of Buddhism was noticeable in India.

(a) Buddhism made the issue of human liberation acceptable to the common people.
(b) The general rules of Buddhism attracted the people.
(c) The path of human liberation or liberation from this life which Buddhism showed to the common people was accepted by all.
(d) Buddhism became acceptable to the Vaishyas and Shudras, known as poor and the lower classes in the society.
(e) Many educational institutions were formed under the influence of Buddhism. In this educational institution, everyone irrespective of caste or creed could get education. Communication and cultural exchange with India developed through Buddhist educational institutions. The contribution of Buddhist educational institutions in this regard cannot be denied.
(f) The Pali language was spread because the Buddhist scriptures were written in Pali.

One of the centres of the spread of Buddhism is in Sanchi, Amravati, Sarnath etc. The spread of Buddhism took place in

Magadha and Kosala in northern and eastern India. Apart from India, Buddhism spread to Sri Lanka during the time of Asoka. The influence of Buddhism was also observed in Myanmar (Burma), Suvarnabhumi (Southeast Asian Peninsula), Macedonia, Kyrgyzstan, Egypt and Syria in North Africa. From the time of Kanishka, Buddhism spread beyond Central Asia to Korea, Bhutan, Japan, Tibet, Sikkim and China.

Jainism

The word 'Jain' comes from the Sanskrit word 'jin'. In Sanskrit, the word 'jin' means 'winner'. The preachers of Jainism were called 'Jains' because they were 'winners'. In his book "Jainism: An Indian Religion of Salvation", Otto Max Helmuth Von Glasenapp called Mahavira a "great hero" while discussing about the Jains. The main theme of Jainism is non-violence and self-control. They adopted non-violence and self-control for salvation and liberation from birth and death. Vilas Adinath commented in his book "Aspects of Jain Religion" that those who transcended addiction, anger, arrogance, greed etc. were called 'Jin'. Through this victory it is possible to attain holy eternal knowledge. Gerant James Lerman commented in his book "Indian Agony over Religion" that the chief religious leader of the Jains was the 'Tirthankaras'. There were 24 Tirthankars. Their education was the main foundation of Jainism. The first Tirthankara was Lord or Rishabhanatha. The 23rd Tirthankara was Parshvanatha or Parshva. The word 'Tirthankara' means the guide to liberation. Mahavira was the last or 24th Tirthankara. Parshvanatha and Mahavira are identified as historical figures.

Parshvanatha or Parshva

According to Jainism, Parshvanatha is the originator of this religion. This is his naming to achieve success in Pareshnath hill. He was the son of the king of Kasi Kshatriya Ashvasena. The advice given by Parshvanatha is known as 'Chaturam'. 'Chaturam' is the four ideologies observed by the Jains.

(a) Non-violence = not killing any animal.
(b) Truth = not lying. That is to behave honestly.
(c) Infallibility = one must not steal anything from others.

(d) Non-acquisition = not owning private property.

The religious institution established by Parshvanatha is called 'Nirgranth'. That is, free from bondage. The 24th Tirthankara gave up his clothes for emancipation.

Mahavira: Brief Introduction

Mahavira ("the great hero") was first known as 'Vardhamana' ("the one who grow"). He was the 24th Tirthankara or the last Tirthankara. He was born in 540 BC at Kundagrama in Vaishali or Kundapur in the kingdom of Videhas. His father's name was Siddhartharaja and his mother was Trishala. Being a child of Kshatriya dynasty, Mahavira was called 'Nayaputta'. From a young age, he was called 'Mahavira' for his brave and fearless character. He was also called 'Muni', 'Samana', 'Nigganth a'. Mahavira took sannyasa at the age of 30. He preferred to be naked in order to be free from all the bonds of the world. After 12 years of pursuit in the village of Jaimbhikagnama on the banks of the river Rijubalika, he attained 'Kevela Jnana' (omniscience, or infinite knowledge) under a sal tree or shorea robusta and became 'Keblin'. This 'Kevala Jnana or Keval gyana' is to become a 'sage' or 'jin' by overcoming various evil sentiments including uncontrolled sexual desire and happiness and sorrow. Mahavira's followers are known as 'Jains' for being 'Jina'. Mahavira traveled to Rajagriha, Champa, Sravasti, Anga, Mithila, Kosala, Gangetic valley and many places in eastern India. Mahavira attained Nirvana (death) near Rajagriha in the town of *Pawapuri* in present-day Bihar in about 468 BC.

Jainism: Five Vows

Mahavira speaks of five vratas (vows) which ascetics and householders must observe. Parshvanatha added this new provision of 'Shuchita' or 'Brahmacharya' with 'Chaturam'.

These ethical principles were preached by Mahavira. These five Vratas (vows) are:

1. Ahimsa (Non-violence or non-injury)
2. Satya (Truthfullness)
3. Asteya (Non-Stéaling)

4. Brahmacharya (Chastity)
5. Aparigraha (Non-attachment)

In his book "Jainism: An Indian Religion of Salvation", Otto Max Helmuth von Glasenap mentions that the followers of Jainism will observe five vows. Jainism emphasized on spiritual awakening through self-control and development of personal consciousness through vows. (1) Mahavira taught that every living being has sanctity and dignity which should be respected as one expects one's own sanctity and dignity to be respected. Ahimsa, Jainism's first and most important vow, applies to actions, speech, and thought. Jains will not harm any living creature. (2) Always vow to speak the truth. Silence is better when truth could cause violence. Applies to oneself and others. (3) Must take a vow not to steal. Not "taking anything that has not been given." (4) Brahmacharya means holiness and abstinence from sex with monks. From the writings of V.D. Mahajan and others, it can be seen that self-control through having sexual activity is 'Brahmacharya'. Abstinence from sex and sexual pleasures for monks, and faithfulness to one's partner for householders. (5) Abstaining from worldly attachments or non-attachment to goods, place, person is highly solicited and required. For lay people, an attitude of non-attachment to property or wordly possessions, for mendicants, not owing anything. Jain monks and nuns perform these five vows with devotion.

The Three Jewels: Triratna

Mahavira thought of getting rid of karma and reincarnation. Salvation means to have eternal happiness. Mahavira found three ways to achieve this liberation. These three paths are collectively called 'Triratna' in Jainism. The three paths are:

(a) *Samyak Darshana* (Right Faith),
(b) *Samyak Gyana* (Right Knowledge), and
(c) *Samyak Charitra* (Right Conduct).

Jainism: Conquering Emotions

In Jainism the emotions of the mind were divided into four parts:

(a) Anger,
(b) Ego,
(c) Misconduct, and
(d) Greed.

According to Jainism, it is possible to conquer these four emotions of the mind. Anger can be conquered through forgiveness, Ego through kindness, wickedness through righteousness, and greed through contentment.

Non-Violence

Paul Dundas mentioned in his book "*The Jains*" non-violence as the main feature of Jainism. Violence is the killing of any living thing. Non-violence was given the most importance in Jainism. Umakanta P. Shah in his book "Jaina-Rupa-Mandana" (Jaina Iconography), commented that the main theme of the non-violence ideology of the Jains is to refrain from practicing non-violence while speaking to oneself, and to refrain from hurting others through work and thought. Non-violence is also shown towards insects in Jainism. Instead of killing them, they were pushed away. Jains (a) adhere to the principle of non-violence towards human beings, (b) animals, (c) insects, and (d) plants. Paul Dundas thinks that Jainism accepts war for the sake of self-defense. However, if a peaceful solution is found, that is the practicable.

Non-Absolutism

They raised the issue of non-absolutism or "Ahimsa, 'Anekantavada" ("many-sideness") in the field of Jainism in Tara Sethia's book "*Ahimsa, Anekantavada and Jainism*". According to Jainism, 'Non-absolutism' is to be free-minded. Its main feature was to accept all kinds of ideologies and to pay homage to different beliefs. According to this doctrine, truth and reality should be judged from different perspectives. Because, judging from a single point of view would always be incomplete.

Jainism: Monasticism

It is known from the writings of Paul Dundas that the practice of asceticism is encouraged and respected in Jainism. Jain monks and nuns live a strict and pious life and practice religion. The observance of the five vratas (vows) of Jainism is considered to be their sole duty. Jains usually wear a piece of white cloth to cover their face so that there is no harm to any insects or germs floating in the air. They clean the road with a broom called 'Rayoharan'. They continue to walk as they sweep the road in front. They also sweep the place to sit so that no insects die under their foot pressure. They practice their monasticism through the principle of non-violence. Paul Dundas said that the presence of nuns in any festival of Jainism is not compulsory.

Jainism: Atma and Karma

Padmanabh S. Jaini in his book "The Jain Path of Purification" commented on Jainism that the innate quality of the soul is holiness. The soul carries its qualities such as

(a) eternal knowledge,
(b) eternal insight,
(c) eternal joy, and
(d) eternal energy in its ideal state.

In reality these qualities are interrupted by the addition of a substance called 'Karma' with the soul. The main goal of Jainism is to liberate the soul completely from the bondage of Karma or action. The ideal or holy state of the soul is also mixed with the impure state of action. Like gold, the soul has to be purified in the right way.

Jainism: Ratnatraya

According to Kailash Chand Jain, three gems are mentioned in Jainism for the salvation of the soul. These three gems are:

(a) Complete knowledge: Gaining accurate knowledge about Jain ideology.
(b) Comprehensive philosophy: The search for the right

insight and truth and at the same time the elimination of superstitions that hinder the way of showing all things clearly.

(c) Complete character: Applying Jain ideals in practical life.

Jainism: The Basic Ideal

According to *Otto Max Helmuth Von Glasenapp*, there are seven basic tenets of metaphysics in Jainism. This is called 'theory'.

(a) Organism: The essence of living matter is called an organism.
(b) Inanimate: Inanimate objects consisting of matter, space, time.
(c) Asrab: The connection of living and non-living things created due to the emergence of the action of the soul.
(d) Confinement: Action binds the living being and deprives the living being of the right to proper knowledge and perception.
(e) Sambar: It is possible to stop the emergence of action by the right character.
(f) Nirjara: Existential action can be avoided through penance.
(g) Salvation: The free soul who has shunned action and has acquired the inherent qualities of holiness, proper knowledge and perception.

Jainism: Svetambara and Digambara

At the end of the fourth century BC, a gathering of Jains took place at Pataliputra. In this assembly Jain scriptures were compiled in 12 parts. At a conference held at *Vallabhi* in Kathiawar, Gujarat in the 5th-6th century BC, these 12 parts were amended and 12 appendages were added. These disciplines are known as 'twelve appendages'. Bhadrabahu's followers did not want to accept this compilation. They strictly obeyed Mahavira's instructions and did not wear any clothes and considered being naked as a way to break free. They are called Digambara. The Jains living in Magadha wore white robes and covered their heads. They were known as Svetambara. The followers of *Sthoolbhadra* were called 'Svetambara'. Although Digambar a men were considered to be entitled to salvation, both men and women of Svetambara were considered to be entitled to salvation.

Jainism: Books

The scriptures of Jainism or Jain Shastras are called 'Jain agam' (Ang Agam Sutras) or 'Jain *Susiddhanta*'. The text on which Mahavira's religious teachings were compiled is 'Kalpasatta' or 'Purva'. The book 'Purva' was divided into 14 volumes. The previous book was revised in 12 volumes in Jain music festival at Pataliputra under the leadership of *Sthulobhadra*. Jain scriptures are called 'twelve Anga'. These were published in 4 parts at the Second Jain Conference at *Vallavi* in Kathiawar. These four parts written in Prakrit language are:

(a) Anga,
(b) Upanga,
(c) Mul and
(d) Sutta.

Spread of Jainism

From Linda's account of Jainism, it can be inferred that Jainism spread to different parts of India. Jainism spread to Kalinga during the Kharavela (Kharabela) period in the first century BC. Jain caves are found in Udayagiri and Khandagiri. The ruins of a Jain temple were discovered in and around Mathura. Ujjain was the main centre of Jainism in western India. Asoka's grandson helped spread Jainism in the southern Andhra and Tamil regions, including *Malav* (Malwa). The Jains took initiative to spread Jainism in South India including Gujarat, Maharashtra and Karnataka on the west coast. Jainism also spread to Hyderabad and Rajasthan.

Buddhism and Jainism: Similarities and Differences

In his book "*Early India: A Concise History*", D.N. Jha found some similarities between Buddhism and Jainism.

(a) Both Gautama Buddha and Mahavira emphasized some mental and physical practices for gaining knowledge. The rigorous practice of Gautama Buddha and Mahavira prove this theory.
(b) Buddhism and Jainism denied the authority of the Vedas.
(c) Buddhism and Jainism opposed animal-based sacrifices. This led to their conflict with conservative Brahmanism.
(d) Buddhism and Jainism took a similar view of trade.
(e) Non-violence was one of the main features of Buddhism and Jainism.
(f) Buddhism and Jainism originated in Eastern India at about the same time.
(g) The proponents of Buddhism and Jainism were people of Kshatriya group.
(h) The spread of Buddhism and Jainism was centred on the lower class people in the urban areas.
(i) There was division in the case of Buddhism and Jainism. Buddhism was divided into two communities, Hinayana and Mahayana. Jainism was divided into two communities, Svetambara and Digambara.
(j) Buddhism and Jainism were the believers in Vedic karma and reincarnation.
(k) In Buddhism and Jainism, emphasis was laid on 'Triratna' i.e. three special qualities. Buddhist Triratna is:
   1. Buddha,
   2. the dharma (doctrine, or teaching) and
   3. the Sangha (the monastic order, or community).

On the other hand, in Jainism the three jewels (also referred to as (natnatnaya) are understood as—

1. *Samyagdarshana* ("right faith"),
2. *Samyagjnana* ("right knowledge"), and 3. *Samyakcharitra* ("right conduct").

One of the three cannot exist exclusive of the others, and all are required for spiritual liberation. (l) In Buddhism and Jainism, the principles of renunciation, adoption of monks and establishment of Sangha were followed. Although there are similarities between Buddhism and Jainism, there are also some differences between the two.

(a) D.N. Jha said that non-violence was important in Buddhism and Jainism. But Buddhism has not completely banned the consumption of non-vegetarian food. The Buddha himself ate meat more than once including beef and pork.
(b) The existence of soul is not acknowledged in Buddhism. The existence of the soul was acknowledged in Jainism. They thought that the soul existed even in inanimate matter.
(c) Gautama Buddha was the first to preach Buddhism. But according to the Jain tradition, 23 more Tirthankars or Jain gurus preached Jainism before Mahavira.
(d) Although the Buddhists completely denied Brahmanism, the Jains did not deny some of its customs or practices. For example, the Jains acknowledged the need for caste. In many cases they also followed Hindu customs.
(e) Strict austerities were emphasized in Jainism.

But in Buddhism, there was talk of adopting or resorting to moderation between luxury and strict austerities. According to D.N. Jha it can be said that neither Buddhism nor Jainism challenged the social norms prevalent at that time. In fact, both religions accepted the caste system. In the Buddhist *Jataka*, it was told that Gautama Buddha could be born only in the upper castes. He can never be born in Vaishya or Shudra caste. As stated in one of the original Jain texts, a Jain Acharya is not born into a low, inferior, fallen, poor, wise or Brahmin family. Buddhism and Jainism, however, did not hinder the lower castes in gaining knowledge.

MAURYA EMPIRE Emergence and Development

8

In the first volume of her book, "A History of India", Romila Thapar identifies the period of the Mauryan Empire as 321 BC to 185 BC. The rise of the Mauryas is an unforgettable chapter in the history of ancient India. Under the Maurya rule, there were vast areas of India except South India. Chandragupta Maurya was the founder of this Maurya dynasty. His period was from 320 BC to 298 BC. Harman Kulke and Dietmar Rothermund, in their book "A History of India", stated that Pataliputra was the capital of the empire, centred on Magadha in the Indus Gangetic plain to the east of the Indian subcontinent.

Maurya Era: Historical Material

Charles River's account of the Maurya period in his book "The Maurya Empire: The History and Legacy of Ancient India's Greatest Empire" is based on a number of historical elements. The historical elements of the Maurya period can be divided into two parts:

(a) Literary material and
(b) Archaeological material.

Literary Material and Archaeological Material

Kautilya's "*Arthashastra*" is one of the most important literary works of the Middle Ages. The details of how the administration functioned in the Maurya period are recorded in this text. Stories of Chanakya

Mauryan Architecture

are told in *Vishakhadatta's* book "Mudrarakshasa". From the book "*Arthashastra*" one can know in detail about the society, economy and state system of Maurya era. Apart from this, the economic and social conditions of the Maurya period are described in Patanjali's book "Mahabhasya". The '*Indica*', written by Megasthenes, the Greek envoy of Alexander's general Seleucus, was significant in understanding the life of the Mauryan society and people. Apart from this book, another important book is "*Indika*" ("Indika")written by Aryan. The Maurya period is also known from the writings of Diodorus, Justin, Plutarch, and Strabo. Although the original text of Megasthenes' "*Indica*" is not available, much information about the administration and society of the Mauryan period can be found in the writings of these Greek writers. According to the German writer Swanbeck, Megasthenes had the correct knowledge and experience about India since he had been in Pataliputra for a long time. Extensive information about the Maurya period can also be obtained from the Buddhist literature "*Divyavadana*", "*Ashokavadana*" and the Buddhist scriptures "Aryamanjusrimulakalpa". Not only literary material, but also archaeological material is an important element to know about the society and administration of Maurya era. Details of the Mauryan Empire can be gleaned from Asoka's inscriptions. Apart from this (a) Junagadh inscription of Rudradaman-I, (b) Girnar inscription and (c) Hathigumpha inscription also gives valuable information about Maurya era and Chandragupta Maurya.

Chandragupta Maurya: Family Identity

Dr. Hemchandra Roychowdhury mentions Chandragupta Maurya as the founder of the Maurya dynasty. According to him, he was the founder of the first large empire in India. The Greek writer Justin in his book "Epitome" mentions Chandragupta Maurya as a child of a gereral lineage. According to Buddhist literature, his period was from 324 BC to 300 BC. In their writings of Hemchandra and Somadeva, Chandragupta Maurya is referred as the son of the Nanda ruler or '*Purvananda Suta*'. In the book '*Parishishta Parvan*', Chandragupta Maurya is described as the child of the daughter of a peacock keeper of a village. Chandragupta Maurya is said to have been born in the 'Moriya' dynasty of Pippalavana in the Terai region of Nepal, according to the texts "*Mahaparinibbana Sutta*" and "*Divyavadana*". The origin of the Maurya dynasty is from this 'Moria' dynasty. According to Brahmanical sources, Chandragupta Maurya was the son of a Shudra woman named Mura. Indirect evidence that the Mauryas were Kshatriyas was found in a Sinhalese source, said S. Chattopadhyay in his book "*Bimbisara to Asoka*".

Chandragupta Maurya: First Life

It is known from various Buddhist literatures that Chandragupta's father Maurya was the ruler of *Pipphalivana*. After the death of his father, Chandragupta's mother took refuge in Pataliputra. Chandragupta Maurya came in contact with Chanakya there. Chanakya noticed the virtues in Chandragupta Maurya and taught him about war, diplomacy, governance etc. Chanakya's "*Arthashastra*" mentions that Chandragupta Maurya included miscreants in his army. Besides, he formed an efficient army with the common people of *Javan*, Kirat, *Shok*, Kamboj etc. communities. With the help of his own skilled army he was able to defeat Nanda king Dhana Nanda of Pataliputra. Books like "*Purana*", "*Mudrarakshasa*" etc. contain details of the conflict of Chandragupta Maurya with Nanda dynasty. It is known from the writings of Justin and Plutarch that Chandragupta Maurya was determined to oust the Nanda dynasty from Magadha early in his political life.

Chandragupta Maurya: Reign and Achievements

In his book "*Hinduism and the Ethics of Warfare in South Asia: From Antiquity to the Present*", Kaushik Roy referred to Chandragupta Maurya as the founder of the Maurya Empire. His reign lasted from 321-297 AD. Roger Boesche commented in his book "*Kautilya's Arthashastra on war and diplomacy in Ancient India*" that Chandragupta Maurya was able to establish a huge empire in the Indian subcontinent. Radhakumud Mukherjee commented in his book "*Chandragupta and the Maurya Empire*" that the first political success of Chandragupta Maurya was the end of Greek rule in north-west India. He first ended Greek rule and overthrew the Nanda dynasty. Dr. Hemchandra Roychowdhury said that Chandragupta Maurya first ousted the Nanda dynasty and later put an end to Greek rule. There were four aspects to his success.

(a) Eviction of the Nanda dynasty,
(b) End of Greek rule in north-west India,
(c) Expansion of the Mauryan Empire, and
(d) Establishment of efficient governance.

According to Dr. Bratindra Nath Mukherjee, Chandragupta Maurya became the owner of a huge empire by destroying the Nanda dynasty. He then went on to expand his empire and clashed with the Greek rulers in northwestern India. Justin's account shows that Euthydemus, Taxilis, Python were all defeated by Chandragupta Maurya. They were all Greek rulers. But the first sign of the political success of Chandragupta Maurya is found in the eviction of the Nanda dynasty by Chandragupta Maurya. According to Radhakumud Mukherjee, Chandragupta Maurya was able to defeat Dhanananda and his general Bhadrasaal and finally besieged the city of Pataliputra and conquered the Nanda Empire in 321 BC at the age of only 20 years.

Chandragupta Maurya: The End of Greek Rule

According to Justin's writings, Seleucus I Nicator was frightened by the colonial invasion of Chandragupta Maurya. Conflict arose between Seleucus I Nicator and Chandragupta. A friendship agreement was also signed between the two. According to Dr. Ranabir Chakravarti, this is probably the first international treaty to which Chandragupta Maurya's name has been associated. According to the writings of Strabo and Plutarch, Chandragupta Maurya gave the Seleucus three regions:

(a) Kabul or Peroperinsdi,
(b) Kandahar or Arakesia, and
(c) Balochistan or Jedrosia.

Dr. Ranabir Chakravarti said there was no evidence that the region of Herat or 'Aria' was given to Chandragupta Maurya. Vincent Arthur Smith in his book Asoka thinks that Chandragupta Maurya was married to Helen, the daughter of Seleucus.

Chandragupta Maurya: South India Expedition

Historian Radhakumud Mukherjee has stated that Chandragupta Maurya invaded South India after his expedition to North and North-West India. He occupied most of the plateau of the Deccan. With the exception of the rest of the Deccan and the Kalinga kingdom, the whole of the Deccan became part of the Mauryan Empire. Upinder Singh said that according to the Tamil poet Mamulanar, the empire of Chandragupta Maurya had spread to the Tirunelveli district of Tamil Nadu. According to the Junagadh inscriptions, the Saurashtra region came under the rule of Chandragupta Maurya. The Sopara region was also associated with it. The areas of Avanti, Uttarapatha, Dakshinapatha, Kalinga etc. were included in the Maurya Empire.

Chandragupta Maurya: Contribution

In agreement with the opinion of Dr. Hemchandra Roychowdhury, we can say that Chandragupta Maurya was the founder of the first historically large empire in India. Apart from Tamil Nadu and Kerala on the south and Chandragupta's empire on the north-east, the empire extended from Kabul, Kandahar in the north-west to Tirunelveli in Tamil Nadu in the south and from Bengal in the east to Saurashtra in the west. He sought help from the Macedonian hero Alexander to oust the Nanda dynasty. Alexander ordered him to be killed instead of helping him. Chandragupta Maurya was not so afraid and formed an efficient army with the republican groups and tribes of Vindhyachal including North-West India. He enlisted the help of his faithful Chanakya to eradicate the Nanda dynasty. He ousted the Greek power. Thus, Chandragupta Maurya established political unity in India.

Bindusara (297-273 B.C.)

According to the Greek writer Strabo, Bindusara was the next ruler of Chandragupta. He took the title "*Amitraghata*" or Amitrochates. The title "*Amitraghata*" means suppressor of the enemy (Sankrit for "Slayer of enemies" or "devourer of enemies"). It is known from the book '*Aryamanjushrimulakalpa*' that Chanakya was also a minister during Bindusara's time. During his reign there was once a revolt in *Takshashila*. He sent his son Asoka, the ruler of *Avanti*, to suppress the rebellion. Asoka was successful in that mission. Although Bimbisara initially took Jain religion, he later converted to Buddhism. According to the Tibetan historian Taranath, he defeated the rulers of 16 cities and gained a huge empire in *Bhimsa*. Like Chandragupta Maurya, he maintained good relations with the kings of Syria and Egypt. He exchanged envoys with King Ptolemy of Egypt and King *Antiochus* of Syria. Bindusara died in 273 BC.

Asoka (273-232 B.C.)

As H.G. Wells comments in his book, "*The Outline of History*", Asoka is the only one of the thousands of rulers in history who is as glorious as a star. It is heard that Asoka was 'Chandashoka' in his early life. He was later converted to 'Dharmashoka'. However, according to Dr. Bhandarkar, there is no evidence that Asoka ascended the throne by killing his brothers. However, the history of Asoka's conflict with Asoka's brother *Sushim* is found. The purpose of Buddhist literature was to propagate the greatness of Buddhism. That is why it was shown how the cruel and violent Asoka became 'Dharmashoka' under the influence of Buddhism. Asoka ascended the throne in 273 BC. However, four years later, in 269 BC, Asoka was anointed as king. According to *Buddhaghosa*, Asoka was a devotee of Hinduism before he converted to Buddhism. According to the historian Kalhan of Kashmir, 'Maheshwar' was the deity of Asoka.

Kalinga War

According to the Buddhist scripture *Divyavadana*, Asoka attacked Kalinga in the eighth year of his inauguration. According to Pliny, the exact reason why Asoka attacked Kalinga has not been recovered from any inscription to date. The reasons behind the invasion of the Kalinga kingdom are various historical speculations as follows:

(a) The Kalinga kingdom became dangerous to the Magadha Empire during the reign of Asoka.
(b) Dr. Bhandarkar thinks that during the reign of Asoka's father Bindusara, the Kalinga kingdom formed an alliance with the Chola and Pandya kings and opposed Bindusara. Asoka saw that the kingdom of Magadha was besieged by the Kalingas in the north and the Cholas and Pandyas in the south. That is why Asoka invaded the Kalinga kingdom.
(c) The invasion and possession of the Kalinga kingdom was inevitable for Asoka for the expansion of the kingdom of Magadha.
(d) At that time the military strength of the Kalinga kingdom continued to increase. The Kalinga kingdom had 60,000 infantry, 100,000 cavalry and 700 war elephants. Asoka invaded the Kalinga kingdom to strike such a strong opponent.

(e) According to Romila Thapar, Kalinga stood in the way of establishing trade relations between South India and Magadha.

In addition, Kalinga was becoming a rival in maritime trade day by day. However, the trade of Magadha had already spread to Burma, Borneo, Bali, Sumatra and Java through the port of Tamralipta. According to Dr. Hemchandra Roychowdhury, the Kalinga war marked a new path in the history of Magadha and India. According to the thirteenth inscription of Asoka, many people died in the battle of Kalinga. The fear of the war made Asoka feel remorse. As a result, he abandoned the war and focused on promoting Buddhism instead of expanding his empire.

Kalinga War: Results

According to Dr. Hemchandra Roychowdhury, the expansion policy he started with the conquest of Bimbisara in Magadha ended in the Battle of Kalinga. As a result of the Kalinga conquest, Asoka's attitude changed. Asoka repented and abandoned Bherighosa (sound of war) or war strategy and concentrated on Dhammaghosha (sound of Dhamma/righteousness) or preaching. It is mentioned in the 6th *Girishasan* that from now on, none of his children, great-grandsons will undertake any new military operation. Asoka adopted religion instead of military campaign after the Kalinga war. Dr. Radhakumud Mukherjee said in his book "Asoka" that the terrible consequences of the Kalinga war had revolutionized Asoka's life. Asoka started his pilgrimage to Gaya in 260 BC. After the battle of Kalinga, he became interested in religion and converted to Buddhism. According to Marxist historian Dr. Romila Thapar, Asoka regretted the fear of the Kalinga war. But even though he repented, he did not return Kalinga's freedom. What he regretted was not done in the Kalinga preaching. But it was preached elsewhere. Asoka did not break up the army or apologize to the rebels as soon as he adopted the religion. According to Dr. Romila Thapar, Asoka abandoned the war strategy because war was no longer needed. The last need of imperialism was fulfilled with the victory of Kalinga. Through the policy of religious conquest, Asoka wanted to strengthen the foundations of the Mauryan Empire without war. According to the Russian Marxist historian Grigory Bongard Levin,

(a) if Asoka truly repented, why was there a gap of four years between the Kalinga war and the propagation of the Thirteenth Inscription? And why was the thirteenth inscription not preached in Kalinga?
(b) It is known from the Kalinga text that even after the conquest of Kalinga, there was a revolt in Kalinga. Asoka, however, suppressed the Kalinga rebellion. Then it was not an example of pacifist policy.
(c) Asoka ascended the throne in 273 BC. He converted to Buddhism between the ages of seven and eleven, before the Battle of Kalinga.

According to Dr. Romila Thapar and Grigory Bongard Levin, Asoka's Kalinga policy was a tool to defend the empire. According to the Marxist historian Damodar Dharmananda Kosambi, it was necessary to abandon the policy of war and adopt a policy of non-violence in order to give a large number of the population of the Mauryan Empire, from North Punjab to Pennar in the south, guaranteed access to agriculture. Thus, Asoka abandoned war politics for economic reasons and adopted religion.

Asoka: Dhamma

Bratindranath Mukherjee thinks that the devotion of the subjects to the king is one of the features of Asoka's Dhamma. Asoka wanted to ensure the loyalty of the people through the propagation of Dhamma. According to Kalhana's book "*Rajatarangini*", Asoka was a devotee of Shaivism till the time of Kalinga war. After the war he became attracted to Buddhism and converted to Buddhism. This dhamma of Asoka is a definite code of conduct morally and spiritually. The word 'dhamma' was first used by Asoka on the minor rock edict of 'Maski'.

Dhamma: Code of Conduct

Radhagobinda Basak, in his book "Asokan Inscription", described

Asoka's inscriptions and columns. The second main pillar is referred to by Asoka as the code of conduct of the Dhamma. The positive aspects of this code of conduct are:

(a) kindness,
(b) generosity,
(c) truth,
(d) purity,
(e) politeness,
(f) The greatest good for the greatest number of people.

Those who would follow this Dhamma were also instructed in certain duties. Such as:

(a) refraining from killing animals,
(b) not harming living creatures,
(c) respecting parents,
(d) respect for elders,
(e) respect for guru,
(f) respect for Brahmins, labourers, friends etc.
(g) low expenditure, and
(h) small savings.

Asoka mentions in his Dhamma some negative aspects which lead to the birth of character defilement and sin. Such as:

(a) Violence,
(b) Cruelty,
(c) Anger,
(d) Ego, and
(e) Jealousy.

Dhamma-followers are told to completely eliminate these issues. It is possible to practice in the right way only by eliminating these. There is also talk of self-criticism to check whether the practice is going in the right direction. Asoka mentions some mental qualities in his Dhamma without which the practice would not be complete. They are—

(a) restraint,
(b) purity of mind,
(c) gratitude etc.

Asoka criticized the ceremony. He spoke of moral conduct in the case of child birth, marriage, etc. Animal sacrifices were forbidden. Asoka said that a person attains eternal virtue through the practice of Dhamma. This eternal virtue is called 'heaven'.

Asoka's Dhamma: Relationship with Buddhism

Historians such as Radhakumud Mukherjee, Dinesh Chandra Sarkar, Devdatta Ramakrishna Bhandarkar are of the opinion that the religion preached by Asoka was in fact Buddhism. In particular, the behaviour of Buddhist householders is the 'Dhamma' preached by Asoka. The features of Asoka's Dhamma were described in "Digha-Nikaya". Gautama Buddha spoke of the ascension of a worldly person. Asoka said the same thing. Historian Devadatta Ramakrishna Bhandarkar considers the Dhamma preached by Asoka to be Buddhism. According to him,

(a) Gautama Buddha prescribed strict rules of conduct for interest. He also prescribed code of conduct for the persons who work within a family. Asoka and his preachers were family man. Asoka preached housework as Dhammaism for the benefit of the people.
(b) The resemblance of Dhamma to Buddhist literature was found. Asoka's dhamma bears a resemblance to the Dhamma described Buddhist principles. Both took the policy of non-violence.
(c) Buddhism did not conflict with Asoka's Dhamma.

The main principles of Buddhism were identified through Dhamma. Dr. Romila Thapar thinks that Asoka tried to gain the support of the people through Dhamma. According to Damodar Dharmananda Kosambi, 'Dhamma' was used as a tool to avoid conflict between different class interests. According to Vincent Arthur Smith,

Dhamma has the essence of all religions but no particular religion. Asoka did not say anything about Buddha or Sangha in his Dhamma. Asoka never mentioned the main issues of Buddhism such as—

(a) Arya Satya,
(b) Astangika Marga (Noble Eightfold Path) or
(c) Nirvana in his Dhamma. Asoka's Dhamma may reflect Buddhism. But Asoka's Dhamma cannot be called Buddhism completely.

According to Thomas William Rhys Davids, 'Dhamma' was not a special religion. Dhamma was told to do what the conscious person should do. Wilson doubted whether Asoka's religion could be called Buddhism. According to Dr. John Faithfull Fleet, Asoka's Dhamma was in fact the principle of duty of pious kings. Romila Thapar in her book "*Asoka and the Decline of the Mauryas*" calls Asoka's Dhamma his own invention. His religion was not Buddhism, though it was influenced by Buddhism and Hinduism. But Asoka made his dhamma a moral and practical way of life. It was easy for the society of that time to follow.

Asoka: Preaching

Asoka's preaching of Buddhism and 'Dhamma' increased the popularity of Buddhism and Dhamma. Asoka's sixth inscription mentions that there is no greater duty to benefit man. The fourth inscription of Asoka's religious scenes awakened religious sentiments among the people. According to the eighth inscription, Asoka started the pilgrimage instead of the pleasure journey. During the time of Asoka, the third Buddhist council was performed at Pataliputra. For the purpose of propagating Dhamma, (a) *Yut*, (b) Rajuka, and (c) Pradeshika etc. employees were appointed. He appointed an employee named "Dhamma *mahamatras*" for preaching and public welfare work. Asoka declared, "All men are my children." He planted trees, dug wells, and made resting places along the highway. According to the 13th inscription, Asoka's envoys went to five Greek kingdoms to preach. These states are:

(a) Syria,
(b) Sirini,
(c) Egypt,
(d) Macedonia, and
(e) Epirus.

He sent his children, brothers and daughters to preach Buddhism in Ceylon. Asoka used to engrave the words on a hill or a stone pillar while preaching the Dhamma. He wanted to build bonds through preaching the religion.

Asoka: Evaluation and Contribution

S. Chattopadhyay in his book "Bimbisara to Asoka" described Asoka as an accomplished and experienced good ruler of the Maurya era. Just as Bimbisara played a role in the rise of the Magadha Empire, so did Asoka in the rise of the Maurya Empire. In his book "*The Chronology of the Reign of Asoka Moriyal*", P.H.L. Eggermont traces the period of Asoka's accession to the throne from 273 BC to 269 BC. According to this text, Asoka converted to Buddhism in 260-59 BC and conquered the kingdom of Kalinga in 261-60 BC. Asoka was the first to preach that the relationship between the king and the subjects was not of the ruler and the ruled, but of the father and the child. He recognized the equal rights of the rich and the poor, the Brahmins and the Shudras in the eyes of the law in eliminating social inequality. According to Vincent Arthur Smith, "Asoka was the first religious leader of mankind". According to world poet Rabindranath Tagore, "Asoka was the greatest emperor in the world". The words of peace, friendship and non-violence were written in the column that Asoka made. Asoka's Dhamma pays homage to religions other than Buddhism. Asoka's contribution to architecture and sculpture is undeniable. Asoka preached the message of universal humanity through the proclamation 'All human beings are my children'. The image of the modern public welfare state can be seen through Asoka's Maurya state. According to Dr. Hemchandra Roychowdhury, 'Asoka had Chandragupta's zeal, Samudragupta's multifaceted talent and Akbar's generosity". According to Damodar Dharmananda Kosambi, "the expansion of the agrarian economy in a peaceful manner was necessary for a large population in the Mauryan Empire". Asoka abandoned his war strategy as a prudent ruler. According to Romila Thapar, "Asoka was not a 'dreamy spiritualist' ruler; he was a realist full-fledged ruler." He was a happy king of the people. He was also the favourite of the gods, *Devanampriyo Priyadarshi*. Romila Thapar, in her book "*Asoka and the Decline of the Mauryas*", said that Asoka's genius and greatness were due to his extraordinary ability to understand the needs of the contemporary person and society and the state along with his needs. Asoka's attitude towards human welfare was very high. Asoka declared in his first column that he would protect people by Dhamma, including observance by Dhamma, provision by Dhamma, making people happy by Dhamma. Asoka has made his regime liberal, welfare-oriented and humane. Asoka's character was a wonderful combination of wisdom and humanity. This is why he is considered as the greatest emperor in history.

Maurya Regime

Vincent Arthur Smith called the Mauryan regime or the Mauryan monarchy 'autocratic'. In the Maurya regime, the king was the central or ultimate authority. He was endowed with uncontrolled power. The Maurya system of government was divided into two parts:

(a) central government and
(b) provincial government.

Central System of Governance

The king was the head of the Maurya regime. The monarchy was founded on strong foundations. Kautilya's "*Arthashastra*" discusses in detail what qualities and qualifications a king needs. The king was the supreme ruler, commander-in-chief, chief justice, and legislator. He was also the head of the military. He also had complete control over the treasury. Although the king had complete freedom to make decisions, he discussed the matter with the cabinet.

(a) Crown Prince,
(b) Priest,
(c) Prime Minister,
(d) Treasurer, and
(e) Chief of Army Staff was a member of the cabinet.

They helped the king with advice on various matters. The king had a significant role in appointing high-ranking officials or bureaucrats. He was also in charge of the army. Those whom Kautilya refers to as "secretaries" in his "Arthashastra" are referred to by Megasthenes in "Indica" as "advisers". In the time of Asoka, among the '*Mahamatras*', those engaged in missionary work were called '*Dharmamahamatras*'. Apart from this, the names of high-ranking persons like 'Shri', 'Principal', 'Mohapatra', 'Anthamahamatra' etc. are found.

Provincial Governance

In the Maurya period the provincial system of government was quite advanced. The number of provinces in that period was:

(a) Uttarapath,
(b) *Takshashila*, which was the capital of the Maurya period,
(c) 'Kalinga', whose capital was 'Tosali',
(d) 'Avantiratta', whose capital was 'Ujjain',
(e) The capital of Dakshinapath was 'Subarnagiri' and
(f) the capital of the East was 'Pataliputra'.

The provincial rulers were divided into two parts. The governorship of these provinces was vested in the 'Kumaras'. Each province was divided into several 'Janapadas'. 'Samaharani' was in-charge of governing this 'Janapada'. The governance of the village was vested in the 'Gramik'. The workers were chosen by the villagers. The upper echelons of the labour force were called 'gop' and were responsible for five to ten villages. There are two types of employees in the provinces:

(a) Antapal: The highest officer of the military management
(b) Durgapal: Security officer of the Fort.

Maurya Rule: Military System

The identity of the Maurya military system is known from the Greek book "*Indica*" by Megasthenes. The Maurya army consisted of 6 lakh infantry, 30,000 cavalry, 6,000 chariots and 9,000 elephants. Kautilya states in his "*Arthashastra*" that there was a 30-member council to manage the military department during the Maurya era. There were a total of 6 associations in this council. Each association had 5 members. These 6 associations are:

(a) infantry,
(b) cavalry,
(c) elephant army,
(d) war chariot force,
(e) navy, and
(f) logistics and vehicle force.

Vincent Arthur Smith praised the military forces of the Mauryan emperor Chandragupta Maurya. Plutarch also praised that with the help of the military, Chandragupta Maurya was able to dominate the whole of India, even to repel the Greek troops and repel the Seleucid invasion. According to Dr. Hemchandra Roychowdhury, Chandragupta Maurya's navy was engaged in suppressing pirates. Vincent Arthur Smith also said that the navy of the Mauryan emperors helped establish relations with foreign countries such as Syria and Egypt.

Maurya Rule: Judiciary

The king was at the top of the Maurya judiciary. He conducted the proceedings with the help of experienced ministers and scholars. Kautilya's "*Arthashastra*" introduces two types of courts. The first is 'Dharmasthiya. The judges of this court were three nobles and three scholars. Civil cases were filed here. The second is 'Kantakasodhana'. There were three nobles and three advocates of this court. Criminal proceedings were held here. There are three types of courts known in "*Arthashastra*".

(a) 'Sangrahan',
(b) 'Dronamukha and
(c) Janapada.

The penal code was strict during the Maurya period. According to "Arthashastra", religion, character and monarchy were considered as laws. Punishment included beheadings, mutilations, and fines. During the reign of Chandragupta Maurya, Brahmins were also severely punished.

The Fall of the Mauryan Empire: Cause

In fact, after Asoka's death in 232 BC, the way was paved for the downfall of the Mauryan Empire. And the fall of this empire was completed in 187 BC when the Mauryan king *Brihadratha* was killed by his general Pushyamitra Shunga. Radheshyam Chaurasia in his book "*History of Ancient India: Earliest Times to 1000 AD*" blamed the weak rulers after Asoka for the downfall of the Mauryan Empire. The weakness of the military power was also responsible for the fall of the Mauryan Empire. In addition, all the factors that were directly related to the destruction of this empire were the opposition of the Brahmanical community, the economic decline and the revolt of the individual nations. The enormity of the empire and the administrative weakness also hastened this fall.

Brahmanical Reaction: Opposition from the Brahmanical Community

Dr. Hara Prasad Shastri said that the hostility of the Brahmanical community towards the Mauryan rule weakened the foundations of Mauryan authority and led to the downfall of the Mauryan Empire. In Magadha, the weak Maurya authority was attacked by the Brahmin general Pushyamitra Shunga, and in Andhra the dominance of the Brahmin Satavahanas was established and the Brahmin *Chet* dynasty occupied Kalinga. Dr. *Hara Prasad Shastri* has put forward several arguments in support of his statement. These statements are as follows:

(a) Asoka was a Shudra king. He stopped animal sacrifices. As a result, the sacrifices of the Brahmins were hindered. As a result, the Brahmins began to express their dissatisfaction against Asoka.

(b) Asoka enacted equal laws for the punishment of criminals. He also stopped discriminating between high and low in terms of usage. As a result, the benefits that the Brahmins had been enjoying in law and justice for so long ceased. As a result, the Brahmins became anti-Asoka.

(c) He struck down the authority of the Brahmins by appointing a royal official named *Dharmamahamatra*.

As a result, the Brahmins took revenge on the weak descendants of Asoka. With the support of the Brahmins, the Buddhist-hating Pushyamitra Shunga killed the last Mauryan king, Brihadratha, and brought down the Mauryan Empire. However, Dr. Hemchandra Roychowdhury could not accept this argument of *Dr. Hara Prasad Shastri*. According to him,

(a) According to Asoka, he was not of Shudra descent. He was a child of Kshatriya dynasty. According to Buddhist and Jain sources, the Mauryas were the descendants of the Kshatriya dynasty called 'Moriya' of *Pippalavana*.

(b) Long before Asoka, animal sacrifices were banned in the *Psalms* and Upanishads.

(c) Asoka did not inflict any harm on the Brahmins by appointing *Dhamma Mahamatras*. One of their duties was to do good to all the people including Brahmins. Brahmins could also be appointed to this post.

(d) The special rights of the Brahmins were not diminished by equality of punishment and equality of use, nor were the Brahmins united with the people of all castes. This introduced similar penalties for Brahmins across the country and similar laws in the courts.

(e) It should also be mentioned that at that time Brahmins did not enjoy any special rights. From the "*Mahabharata*", "*Arthashastra*", etc., it is known that Brahmins accused of treason were drowned.

(f) Although Pushyamitra Shunga was a Brahmin, he was a Buddhist hater; no evidence of this is available.

Based on the views of *Dr. Hara Prasad Shastri* and Dr. Hemchandra Roychowdhury, Grigory *Bongard Levin*, with the help of anecdotes such as *Sutralankara, Asokavadana*, etc., showed that Asoka was biased towards Buddhism at the end of his reign. Asoka spent a lot of money on the propagation of Buddhism and the construction of Buddhist monasteries. This is why the Brahmanical reaction began. Referring to Asoka's first small Girishasan, E. Senert said, "He has falsified the Brahmins, who were supposed to be gods."—Asoka's announcement angered the Brahmins. As D.C. Ahir commented in his book "*Asoka The Great*", Asoka was the first Buddhist emperor in the history of India and his various anti-Brahmin activities paved the way for the downfall of the Mauryan Empire.

Economic Crisis

Many historians have identified the economic crisis as one of the main reasons for the downfall of the Mauryan Empire. *Ranabir Chakravarti* thinks that the money that was earned from the revenue did not make it possible for the economic development of this huge empire. This led to the downfall of the Mauryan Empire. Dwijendra Narayan Jha and Romila Thapar think that the money that was available from the agricultural revenue in the Maurya period could not (a) support a large army and (b) pay for Asoka's religious work. According to Damodar Dharmananda Kosambi, in those days unnecessary taxes were levied in some cases, such as: taxes on actors and prostitutes. It is understood that this tax was introduced to revive the economy. However, according to Dwijendra Narayan Jha, the decline of the economy in the Maurya era was the main reason for the downfall of this empire. This is because the amount of silver in the coin found in the Maurya period declined sharply towards the end, which is a sign of economic decline. In conclusion, although agricultural expansion took place in the Gangetic valley, it was not ubiquitous in the empire and it was not possible for the growing agricultural economy in certain areas to meet the growing costs of the vast empire.

Rebellion and Tyranny of the Provincial Rulers

Dr. Hemchandra Roychowdhury in his book "*The Political History of Ancient India*" blamed the tyranny of the provincial rulers for the downfall of the Mauryan Empire. At that time *Dharmamahamatra* and Rajukas became more powerful. As their oppression continued to increase, it became a cause of dissatisfaction among the people. The king also failed to control these provincial rulers. However, the tyranny of the nobility in the remote provinces and the consequent revolt of the people in the provinces started from the time of Bindusara. During the reign of Bindusara, there was a revolt in *Takshashila*. The cause of the downfall of the Maurya Empire is mentioned in the book "*Divyavadana*". The Kalinga inscription shows that Asoka forbade his servants to oppress the people without any reason. From this it can be inferred that at that time the provincial rulers used to oppress the common people. This led to chaos in the Mauryan Empire. The rebellious people are said to have left the provincial empire and declared independence.

Rebellion of Different Races

During the time of Asoka, the distinctness and power of unique races and tribes was recognized. Asoka recognized the uniqueness and sovereignty of these distinct races. Notable among these races were:

(a) Pulind,
(b) Kamboj,
(c) Andhra,
(d) Veje,
(e) Chola,
(f) Rashtrik,
(g) Pandya,
(h) Keralaputra, and
(i) Satyaputra.

After the death of Asoka, these individual races became stronger and helped in the downfall of the Mauryan Empire.

The Enormity of the Mauryan Empire

The enormity of the Maurya Empire is one of the reasons for the downfall of this empire. In the Maurya era, there was no facility to travel from one place to another very easily and quickly. Due to the difficulty of establishing communication everywhere in the empire, the central monarchy could not maintain equal dominance everywhere. This led to the downfall of the Mauryan Empire.

Administrative Weakness

Administrative weakness in the Mauryan Empire was one of the reasons for the downfall of the Mauryan Empire. In the Maurya period, the rulers used to appoint subordinates as per their wishes. Thus, skilled and suitable employees were not employed. As a result of the recruitment of staff from the regional social groups, the regional administration would act accordingly to the interest of that regional group. The social administration of the empire was weakened due to the lack of specific policies to control the different social and regional groups. The espionage system in the Maurya period started unrest in the political and administrative spheres of the empire. According to Romila Thapar, administrative weakness caused problems in the political and administrative spheres.

The Weakness and Incompetence of the Next Rulers

According to Kalhana's book "*Rajatarangini*" ("River of Kings"), after Asoka's death, Birsen declared independence in Kashmir and extended his kingdom to Kannauj. According to Taranath, *Jalauk* declared independence in Kashmir. The weakness of Asoka's successors played a supporting role in the downfall of the Mauryan Empire. The weakness and rivalry of the later emperors of Asoka was the cause of the downfall of the Mauryan Empire. According to Dr. Hemchandra Roychowdhury, no worthy emperor was seen after Asoka. As a result, the empire was weakened and the Maurya Empire collapsed.

Asoka's Responsibility

Dr. Ramakrishna Gopal Bhandarkar commented in his book "Asoka" that as a result of morality, the military side gradually became reluctant among the people. As a result, the decline of the Mauryan Empire was also severely affected. According to Dr. Hemchandra Roychowdhury, Asoka was responsible for the downfall of the Mauryan Empire. His theology contributed to this downfall. Asoka abandoned the war policy and adopted the Dhamma policy, which weakened the military base of the Maurya Empire. Asoka took measures so that no one in the dynasty could adopt a war strategy. Without military power, the Mauryan Empire would not have survived for long. That is why Asoka's policy is blamed for the downfall of the Mauryan Empire. According to Dr. Radhakumud Mukherjee, if Asoka could have maintained his military policy and kept the army active, the Mauryan Empire could have expanded much more. Thus, Asoka's responsibility for the downfall of the Mauryan Empire cannot be denied.

SATAVAHANA PERIOD (230-220 BC)

9

After the fall of the Mauryan Empire, the unity of India was temporarily ruined. At this point the foreign invasion began. Although South India was completely free from foreign rule. During this period the Satavahanas established an empire in Maharashtra and Andhra Pradesh in southern India. The Satavahanas built a long-lasting empire there. This empire lasted for about 400 years. The Satavahanas emerged after the fall of the Mauryan Empire. Ramashankar Tripathi commented in his book "*History of Ancient India*" that according to the Puranas, 'Andhra' and 'Satavahana' were the names of the same dynasty. But the Satavahanas did not identify themselves as 'Andhra'. The Satavahanas did not even use the name 'Andhra' in their inscriptions. The Satavahanas conquered Andhra Pradesh after expanding their dominance in

Coins of Satavahana Dynasty

the Deccan. Due to the separation of the northern and western regions, the political power of the Satavahanas was maintained in the area between the Godavari and Krishna rivers. From then on, the Satavahanas became known as 'Andhra'. 'Andhra' and 'Satavahana' belong to the same dynasty, so this dynasty can also be called 'Andhra-Satavahana'. The Satavahanas formed a large empire centred on present-day Maharashtra and Andhra Pradesh. In the Puranas, the Satavahanas were called 'Andhra' and 'Servant of Andhra'. Dr. K. Rajagopalachari in his book "A Comprehensive History of India" called him a servant of the country. Durgaprasad in his book "History of the Andhras upto 1565 BC" mentions that the Mahapurana states that Andhra or Satavahanas had 29 kings and a total reign of 460 years.

Historical Material

Much information on the political history of the Satavahanas is available from the "*Matsya Purana*" and the "*Vayupurana*". Apart from this, other importants documents for writing the history of Satavahana dynasty were various puranas and "*Brihatkatha*", a book written by Gunadhya. Dr. K. Gopalachari mentions (a) Ptolemy's "Geography", (b) Pliny's "Natural History", and (c) Anonymous author's "Periplus of the Erythrian Sea" as important elements of historiography of the Satavahana period. The coin found by Dr. Bratindranath Mukherjee gives an idea of the economic condition of the Satavahana period. Notable inscriptions of the Satavahana period were Nanaghat or Naneghat inscription written by the wife of Satakarni-I, Nayanika and Hatigumpha inscription. Apart from this, the history of Satavahanas is known from the coins found at Nasik, Kondapur.

Satavahana Era: The Kings of the First Era

Dr. Hemchandra Roychowdhury in his book "The Political History of Ancient India" mentions Simuka as the founder of the Satavahana dynasty. It is known from the writings of George Buhler and James Burgess that Simuka is mentioned in the Nanaghat inscription as the founder of the Satavahana dynasty. Vidisha and the surrounded regions of Vidisha were included in his empire. The period of Simuka was 100-70 BC. H.H. Wilson translated "The Vishnu Purana" edited by Fritz Ward. This text is believed to have different names in different Puranas as the founder of the Satavahana dynasty. Such as: Shishuka in "*Matsya Purana*", Sipraka in "*Vishnu Purana*", Sindhuka in "*Vayu Purana*" Chhesmaka in "*Brahmanda Purana*" and Shudraka or Smaka in Kumarika Khanda of "Skanda Purana" etc. Simuka was a feudal lord under the Kanvas and overthrew the Kanvas and established the Satavahana dynasty. Kanha was the ruler of the Satavahana dynasty after Simuka. Its time is 60-70 BC. Satakarni-I was the next ruler of the Satavahana dynasty. He ruled in the Deccan of India. During his reign the expansion of the Satavahana Empire was noticed. During his reign the Satavahana Empire spread to the Godavari valley. Paithan on the banks of Godavari was his capital. In the Nanaghat inscription of Nayanika (Naganika), Satkarni-I was called 'Dakshinapath Pati'. According to Rajesh Kumar Singh, the reign of Satakarni or Satakarni-I was 187-177 BC. He performed the rajsuya yajna in the first century BC. Sivasvati reigned after the Satakarni-I. He ruled for 28 years. He occupied Pune and Nasik. North Maharashtra and the Vidarbha region were also included in his empire.

Gautamiputra Satakarni (106-130)

In his book "Empires Perspectives from Archeology and History", Susan E. Alcock states that Gautamiputra Satakarni, the ruler of the Satavahana dynasty, ruled in the Deccan of India. He ascended the throne 100 years after the death of the Satakarni-I. He was the greatest king of the Satavahana dynasty. However, there are differences of opinion about his reign. Some say he was on the throne from 86 AD to 110 AD. According to many, this period is 103-127 AD. According to Rajesh Kumar Singh, Gautamiputra Satakarni ruled from 106-130 AD. According to his mother Gautami Balashri's 'Nashik Prashasti', Gautamiputra took over Maharashtra from the Satakarni Sakas. He also won against the Yavanas and the Pahlavas. Raghunanda Rao commented in his book "*History and Culture of Andhra Pradesh: From the Earliest Times to the Present Day*" that Gautamiputra Satakarni ascended the throne at a critical time in the Satavahana Empire.

Gautamiputra Satakarni: Political Achievement

According to the Nashik (eulogy) Prashasti, Gautamiputra Satakarni is mentioned as the slayer of Saka, Yavana and Pahlavas. Sakas here refer to Sakas from Central Asia. It is in this Nashik Prashasti (eulogy) that Gautamiputra Satakarni has been referred to as the drank water of these three oceans i.e.

(a) The Indian Ocean,
(b) the Arabian Sea, and
(c) the Bay of Bengal. That is why he is hailed as 'Trisamadradisvara'.

The Nashik Prashasti mentions 14 conquests of Gautamiputra Satakarni:

(a) The region between Godavari and Krishna 'Asika' (area of Godavary valley),
(b) Asmaka (Ashmaka) in Godavari valley,
(c) Mudhaka or Mulaka (area around paithan),
(d) Surastha (Saurashtra),
(e) The northern region of Kathiawar or Kukura,
(f) Narmada South Region or Ancient Mahishmati or Anupa (area around Mahishmati in Narmada Valley),
(g) Vidarbha (Berar) of present Nagpur,
(h) Adjacent to Vidisha and Avanti-Ujjain,
(i) Vindhya mountain to the north of Narmada, and
(j) Purbaghat or Mahendra,
(k) Akara-Avanti (eastern and western Malwa) etc. region.

According to Dr. Dinesh Chandra Sarkar, after Vindhyachal, his sovereignty was also maintained in South India. According to Nashik Prashasti, he defeated Nahapana and called himself a Saka killer. According to Dr. Bratindranath Mukherjee, Gautamiputra Satakarni maintained his dominance in the Deccan. He took the titles of 'Rajadhiraja', 'Rajaraja' etc.

The Achievement of Gautamiputra Satakarni

Gautamiputra Satakarni was described by Dr. Sanjeev Kumar Tandel as the most powerful and great ruler of the Satavahana dynasty in his book "Indian History". His empire extended from Malwa in the north to Konkan in the south. He crushed the arrogance of the Kshatriyas and established the lower class people in social status. He also defended the interests of the Brahmin class. He is the founder of Benaktak town in Govardhan district. Sohei Ichimura in his book "*Buddhist Critical Spirituality: Prajna and Sunnyata*" mentions the contribution of Gautamiputra Satakarni in the field of Buddhism. With his help, many Buddhist caves were built at Amravati and Nagarjunakonda. Gautamiputra Satakarni donated caves and land for the people of Buddhism in places like Nashik and Carle. In the case of architecture and art of the Satavahana period, therefore, Buddhist stupas and Buddhist monasteries were significant. Gautamiputra Satakarni was an advanced warrior. Tax reforms were carried out during his tenure. Trade with West Asia and Rome increased under his able guidance.

Vasisthiputra Sri *Pulamavi* (130-159 A.D.)

According to the Puranas, *Puloma* was the successor of Gautamiputra Satakarni, who is believed to be identical with Vasisthiputra Sri *Pulamavi*. According to this myth, he ruled for 21 years. Vasisthiputra Sri Pulamavi was also known as Nandiniputra Sri *Pulamavi*. According to Ptolemy, Paithan was the capital of Pulamavi. It is known from the inscriptions found at Amravati that his kingdom was bounded by the mouth of the river Krishna. The Pandava cave was built by Queen Gautami Balashri during the *Pulamavi* period. Unique patterns of architecture is also seen there. According to Dr. Hemchandra Roychowdhury, the reign of Vasisthiputra Sri *Pulamavi* lasted from 130 to 154 AD. During his time maritime trade flourished. The empire of *Pulamavi* spread to Madhya Pradesh and the Karmandal coast. As he was married to the daughter of Rudradaman-I, a king of the Sakas. That is why Rudradaman-I invaded the Satavahana kingdom but did not destroy it. Then Vasisthiputra Satkarni, Shivaskanda Satakarni reigned. It is believed that Pulamavi died in 158 AD.

Yajnasri Satakarni (165-196 A.D.)

Prannath Chopra in his book "Encyclopedia of India" mentions Yajnasri Satakarni as 'Gautamiputra Yajnasri'. There is a disagreement about his duration and tenure. Ramashankar Tripathi in his book "*History of Ancient India*" mentions the period of Yajnasri Satakarni as 165-196 AD. He emerged as the last powerful king of the Satavahana dynasty. He ruled over Maharashtra and Andhra Pradesh. From the Sakas he inherited the the region Aparanta Kanho. Many silver coins of his time were found at Suppara (Sopara), the capital of Aparanta. North Konkan was inherited from the descendants of *Rudradaman-I*. During the time of Yajnasri Satakarni, the naval power of the Satavahanas increased. After the death of Yajnasri Satakarni, the Satavahanas became weak. The dominance of the Satavahana eroded gradually because of the rise of the (a) Vakataka, (b) Ikshwaku and (c) Pahlavas.

Satavahana Era: Material Culture

Material culture spread in the Satavahana era. The Satavahanas used iron ore from Karimnagar and Warangal region. High quality (a) spade, (b) plow blade, (c) axe, (d) razor, and (e) shovel etc. used at that time was found. The Kolar gold mine was discovered during the Satavahana period. The Satavahanas introduced coins of copper and bronze. They also used gold butts or bullion.

Expansion of Agriculture

During the Satavahana period, the agro-economy was greatly expanded and improved. The reason behind this improvement is that at that time a lot of paddy was cultivated in the basin of Krishna and Godavari Rivers. Naturally it is understood that the Satavahanas were fully aware of the method of cultivation. Apart from paddy, the Satavahanas also showed skill in the production of cotton or cotton products. Evidence of improved irrigation system was also found at that time. As a result, a kind of rural economy flourished in the Deccan during the Satavahana period.

The Rise of the City

The rise of city culture is evident in the Satavahana Empire. The use of burnt bricks and perforated tiles can be noticed in Karimnagar area. Patterns of underground sewers can also be noticed in this era. The rise of the city during the reign of the Satavahanas can be traced back to Pliny's writings. This empire was densely populated. It is also known from Pliny's writings that in addition to many villages in the Andhra Pradesh region, there were 30 fortified cities. Notable among the cities on the west coast were—

(a) Nashik,
(b) Govardhanagar, and
(c) Vaijayanti etc.

Society and Culture of Satavahana Era

The predominance of Brahmanism was found during the Satavahana period. Gautamiputra Satakarni considered himself a Brahmin and mentioned 4 classes in the society. He formed 4 social classes according to the profession. Although the Satavahanas identified themselves as Brahmins, they fought and ruled the country like the Kshatriyas. Gautamiputra Satakarni married his child to the princess of Saka. At this time it was not possible to accept the strictness of caste system. The main reason for this is the spread of Buddhism. Another reason is the arrival of Saka, *Pahlavas* etc. in South India. Moreover, the Satavahana kings, though adherents of the Brahmanical religion of northern India, could not deny the custom of the indigenous tribes of the south. As a result, tribal culture was mixed and integrated with Brahmanical culture. Women were given more importance in the Satavahana society. The practice of naming children after mothers was common. Gautamiputra Satakarni was named after his mother. In addition, during religious ceremonies, women or wives get the status of suitable social or consort. In the book '*Gathasaptasati*' the dignity of women has been mentioned during the Satavahana period. The women were skilled in music and dance. They also had a deep interest in poetry. They had been taught all these things since childhood. Sanskrit literature spread during the time of Gautamiputra

Satakarni, *Pulamavi* Yajnashri Satakarni. In the Satavahana period, excellent examples of architecture and sculpture were found. Apart from this, patterns have been found in Chaitya, Bihar and Stupa. Evidence of the construction of a temple was found by cutting down a hill in the cave chaitya of Carl. Inscriptions of Gautamiputra Satakarni are inscribed in the monasteries discovered at Nashik. Many mounds were discovered in the Amravati regions which are believed to have been rebuilt during the Satavahana period. In the Satavahana era, '*Brahatkathamanjari*' was written in Prakrit language. In this text the social condition of the Satavahana era can be noticed. Dr. K. Rajagopalachari considers Hall to be a culture conscious person.

Satavahana Era: Governance

In his book "*Some Early Dynasties of South India*", Sudhakar Chattopadhyay, while discussing the constitutional system of the Satavahanas, mentioned two aspects of governance. On one side were the royal staffs, on the other the provincial staffs. Satavahana was a combination of the qualities of the kingdom of gods like King Rama, Bhima, Keshab, Arjuna. Satavahana Commander was the provincial ruler. 'Gaulomika' was in charge of maintaining law and order in the countryside. Under him were 9 chariots, 9 elephants, 25 horses and 45 infantry. During the Satavahana period, the districts were known as 'Ahar'. The officials of 'Ahar' were 'Amatya' and 'Mahamatra'. Progress in the feudal military field was noticed in the provincial system of governance. Dr. K. Rajagopalachari called the Satavahana Empire a 'Police State'. The Satavahanas introduced land donation to Brahmins and Buddhists. In the early days of this land donation system, revenue was not collected from the lands. The donor was later given administrative powers. Gautamiputra Satakarni forbade his bureaucrats to interfere in the administrative work of the donated land and the village. According to Ramsharan Sharma, Buddhist monks used to advise respect for political authority. Besides, they used to spread the message of peace among the common people. It is worthy of mention that the condition of the peasants was not generally prosperous during his reign. Farmers were exploited heavily due to feudal system. There were three levels of feudalism or three-tier feudalism in the Satavahana regime. The king was supreme and he could issue coins. 'Mahabhojgon' was on the second tier. Ramsharan Sharma in his book "*Aspects of Political Ideas and in Ancient India*" praised the rule of Satvahanas. Later imitations of this regime were noticed in the other antecedent dynasties. The revenue system was not strict at all during the reign of this dynasty.

Satavahana Era: Trade

Charles Hisshaus, in his book "*Encyclopedia of Ancient Asian Civilization*", raised the issue of trade in the success and dominance of the Satavahanas. The Satavahanas prospered heavily in trade with the West at that time. The trade of the Satavahanas with the Roman Empire is known from various sources. During the Satavahana dynasty, foreign trade flourished in the Krishna-Godavari region. The Sangam literature states that ships from the west would bring gold coins to the port of *Machilipatnam* and return home with pepper instead. Roman pottery, goblets, lamp stands, and wooden vessels from the first and second centuries AD have been discovered. During the reign of the Roman Emperor Augustus, envoys were sent to Rome from *Barygata* or Bharneh in the western Deccan. According to Charles Hisshaus, the book "Periplus on the Erythrian Sea" mentions Rome's trade relations with the Satavahanas, and Pliny's writings deal with the rich trade with Rome. Apart from *Brouch*, during the time of Satavahanas, there were prosperous ports (a) *Sopara* and (b) Kalyan. Gold, silver, lead, glass, copper, tin, coins, etc. were imported from India during the Satavahana period. Buddhist monasteries also provided financial support for internal and external trade. During the reigns of Vasisthiputra Sri *Pulamavi* and Yajnasri Satakarni, the Satavahanas prospered in the commercial field. Raoul McLaughlin described the commercial port of Kalliena for the Satavahanas.

Satavahana Era: Religious Atmosphere

B.S.L. Hanumantha Rao in his book "*The Religion in Andhra: A Survey of Religious Developments in Andhra from Early Times upto AD 1325*" thinks that the first Satavahana ruler among the Satavahana rulers was a patron of Jainism. The author's other book, "*The Age of Satavahanas*", discusses the Satavahanas' special devotion to Jainism and Buddhism. The Satavahanas identified themselves as Brahmins and became enthusiastic about the spread of Brahmanism in the Deccan. In fact, the Satavahana kings were adherents of Vedic Hinduism. In Nashik Prashasti, Gautamiputra Satakarni is mentioned as one of the unique among the Brahmins. B.S.L. Hanumantha Rao also said that Vaishnava deities were the deities of the Satavahanas. Such as: Krishna-Basudev. Mahayana Buddhism was influential during the Satavahana period. Nagarjunakonda and Amravati were one of the notable centres of Buddhist culture during the Satavahana period. The Satavahana rulers performed Rajsuya Yajna and Vajapeya Yajna. Gauri Puja and Pashupati Puja are identified in the book "*Gathasaptasati*" written by the Satavahana ruler Hall. (a) Sun (b) Moon (c) Worship of natural deities like Indra was prevalent in Satavahana era. 134 Buddhist caves were built at Junnar, the second capital of the Satavahanas. Pidatala Sitapati and V.V. Krishna Shastri, in their writings, referred to the Vedic and Brahmanical sects of the Satavahanas as a religious feature of the Satavahanas which created a religious atmosphere in the Deccan. Niharranjan Roy said in his book "*History of Bengalis: Early Episodes*" that the South had been a major centre of Brahmanical religion and culture since the Satavahana period.

THE SANGAM ERA 10

The Sangam era has a special significance in the history of India, specifically in South India. T.V. Mahalingam in his book "*Kanchipuram in Early South Indian History*" expressed the view that there was a great improvement in Tamil literature during the Sangam era. The history of the Sangam period is the history of ancient Tamil Nadu and Kerala i.e. 'Tamilkam'. Its range is from 500 BC to 300 BC. P.T. Srinivas Iyengar in his book "*History of the Tamils from the earliest times to 600 AD*" commented that the ancient Tamil language was known as 'Tamilakam'. Sangam literature developed in the ancient Tamil-speaking regions, namely Tamil Nadu, Kerala, Andhra Pradesh and parts of Karnataka in southern India, and in northern Sri Lanka or the 'Eelam' region.

Sangam Literature

Kamil Javenabil commented in his book "*The Smile of Murugan on Tamil Literature of South India*", according to Tamil legend there were 3 Sangams:

(a) The first Sangam period,
(b) The second Sangam period or middle sangam period, and
(c) The third Sangam or the third Academy.

In his book "*A Brief History of India*", Alain Daniello comments that the first Sangam lasted for 4440 years. The second Sangam lasted 3700 years. He mentioned that the third Sangam lasted for 1850 years. Sangam literature is the earliest stage of Tamil literature. Many Tamil poets composed their poems at this stage of Sangam literature. The poems were later formally recognized by the '*Kabi*' group or Kavi-Parishad. The word 'Sangam' was derived from a Dravidian word. The word sangam was used in the sense of society, group, association or council. It was called Sangam as the Council of Poets came together and formally recognized this Tamil literature. Sangam literature was a part of classical Tamil literature. In his book "*A History of South India*", Kallidaikurichi Aiyah Nilakanta Sastri traces the period of Sangam literature from 300 BC to 600 BC. According to El Hart George's "*The Poems of Ancient Tamil*", Sangam literature was a collection of 2681 poems written by 473 poets. According to Irayaner, the content of Sangam literature was secular and the details of daily life of Tamils were the main content of Sangam literature. Sangam literature again became popular after getting rediscovered by C.W. Tamotarampillai and U.V. Swaminatha Ayyar in the nineteenth century.

The First Sangam Period

The famous Tamil commentator of the Sangam era Nakkirar mentioned three Sangams. The first Sangam took place in the ancient city of Madurai. Mahamuni Agastaya or Agathiyar was the president of the first Sangam. The number of the members of the first Sangam was 549. The poems of 4499 poets were approved. The Pandya kings patronized the first Sangam. There were 9 poets among the Pandya kings. The first Sangam lasted 4440 years. Among the collections of poems of the first Sangam, (a) *Kalariyavirai*, (b) Madunarai, (c) Perumpari-padal, and (d) Mudukuruku were important. William Herman commented that among the members of the first Sangam were gods like Murugan, Shiva, Kuperan.

The Second Sangam Period

Alain Danielou, while introducing the second Sangam, remarked that the second Sangam took place in the town of Kapatapuram. The duration of the second Sangam was 3700 years. 59 members and 1700 poets participated in the second Sangam. The members of the second Sangam were:

Agastyar and ancient Tamil scripts (Temple walls of Tunjore Bragadeeshwara temple

(a) Irundayur,
(b) Kurungolimosi,
(c) Bellurkapion, and
(d) Agastya.

59 Pandya kings patronized the second Sangam. 8149 books were preserved in the library of the organization of the second Sangam. Notable among the collections of poems that were composed in the second Sangam are:

(a) Kurunthogai,
(b) Sirrisai,
(c) Perisai,
(d) Paripaadal,
(e) Kuttu,
(f) Vari,
(g) Kali,
(h) Netunthogai,
(i) Kurunthogai,
(j) Nanooru,

(j) Narrihai Nanooru,
(k) Purananooru,
(l) Aingurunooru, and
(m) Padirrupaatu.

Apart from this, grammar books such as—

(a) Agattiyam and
(b) Tholkappiyam were written in the second Sangam.

The Third Sangam Period

Edward Jewitt Robinson mentioned many accounts of the third Sangam in his book "*Tamil Wisdom: Traditions Concerning Hindu Sages and Selection from their Writings*". According to him, the third Sangam took place in the town of North Madurai. It lasted for 1800 years. 449 members and 49 Pandya kings were patrons of this Sangam. The last part of the book "Tirukkural" (Kural) written by Valluvar or Thiruvalluvar mentions the names of the members of the third Sangam. Notable among the poets of this third Sangam were:

(a) Kapilar,
(b) Panamparanar,
(c) Iraiyanar,
(d) Seethalai Sathanate,
(e) Nakkirar, and
(f) Pandya king Ugra etc.

There are doubts as to whether Chithalai Chathanar, the author of "Manimekalai", was a poet of the Sangam era. Among the collections of poems composed in the third Sangam of Iraiyanar are—

(a) *Nedunthoke*,
(b) *Kurunthokai*,
(c) *Natrinai*,
(d) *Paripadal*,
(e) *Kuthu*,
(f) *Nari*,

(g) *Perisai*,
(h) *Sitrisai*, and
(i) *Ainkurunukur*.

According to Iraiyanar's description of the three Sangams, the Sangams lasted for 9950 years. Generally, the Sangam era ended in 300 or 500 AD. Then Sangam literature must have started in S250 or 9450 BC. There are doubts about the duration of the Sangam era. But the idea of the period of Sangam era for 10,000 years is not historically plausible. Many of the three deities of Iraiyanar were considered members. Whatever Iraiyanari's statement, Sangam literature was a significant literary achievement from the historical point of view of ancient India.

Sangam Literature: Three Parts

According to Srinivas Iyengar, the Sangam literature was huge. The size of Sangam literature also increased as it was a place of shelter for many poets. Iyengar spoke of three parts of Sangam literature. These three parts are:

(a) Pattuppattu or the ten Idylls or Ten Lays,
(b) Ettuttokai or The Eight Anthologies or "Eight Collections" and
(c) Patinenmel Kanakku or The Eighteen Greater Texts.

Thiruvalluvar's famous book "Tirukkural" or "Kural" was one of the eighteenth principles poetry books. The book titled 'Kural' introduces the thoughts, hopes and aspirations, happiness and sorrows of human life. Pattuppattu and Ettuttokai are considered to be the main ones in the field of Sangam literature. Eighteenth principle poems are in many cases not accepted as Sangam literature.

Pattuppattu or The Ten Idylls or Ten Lays

Nakkirar contributed two poems in the ten descriptive poems.

(a) Tirumurukannuppatai ("Guide to Lord Murugan"), and
(b) Netunalvatai ("Good Long Northern Wind).

The first poem, 'Tirumurukarruppatai', is a praise of the god Murugan. The description of the temples in which the god Murugan was worshipped is found in this poem. In the poem 'Netunceliyan' by Nakkirar, the separation of King 'Netunalvatai' and his queen is described. As a result of King Netunceliyan being on the battlefield, the queen is left alone in the palace. The main theme of the poem was the anguish of the king and queen and the deep love between them. Kasiyalur Uruthirankannanar is a famous poet of the Sangam era. One of the most notable poems written by him is 'Perumpanatruppadai'. The stanza number of this poem is 500. The description of the city of Kanchipuram is found in this poem. Another notable poem is Paltinappaalai. In this poem of love and affection, it is seen that the hero is responsible to his lover. The hero was called to join the war. But the hero chose emotion instead of duty in recognition of his love and affection. Srinivas Iyengar thinks that the importance of the ten descriptive poems or Pattupattu is immense. The fanmous poet named Maruthana wrote an important poem named Mudurai Kaanchi. This poem contains a description of Netunceliyan's empire. One of the poems written by Mudatthamak Kanniyar is 'Porunaraatruppadai'. This poem describes the poverty of the poets of the Sangam era. The poem written by Nallur Nathathathanar is 'Sirupanatruppadai'. This poem describes the various qualities of the character of King Nalliyakkotan. Nalliyakkotan was mentioned as the ideal character in the kingdom. In Napputhunar's poem 'Mullaippattu', the queen's longing for her expatriate husband is described. The queen was losing patience with her husband's thoughts. The queen once heard the news of her husband's return. Kapilar's poem 'Kurincippattu' reveals the love affair between a chief of hill and a beautiful lady. Despite many obstacles in their way of marriage, they eventually tied the knot. Perunkousikanar poem 'Malaipatukataam' contains a beautiful description of natural beauty.

Ettuttokai or The Eight Anthologies or "Eight Collections"

Ettuttokai or eight collections of poems were composed of high quality literature. The aspect of Tamil social system was also reflected in those poems. There are hints of some short lyric poems in only one of the eight anthologies.

(A) The first collection is Natrinai which is a collection of 400 lyric poems.
(B) The second collection 'Kuruntokai' is 400 poems of love.
(C) The third collection 'Ainkurunuru' is a collection of 500 romantic poems. Five forms of love can be seen in the poems of this stage. These five stages are
  (a) reunion,
  (b) waiting,
  (c) arrogance,
  (d) separation, and
  (e) mourning.
(D) The fourth collection 'Patirruppattu' is a collection of poems of ten stanzas. These poems express entertainment, women's hairstyles and the characteristics of the *Chera* kings. One of the female poets of this period is Kakkai Pudiniyar.
(E) The fifth collection is 'Paripatal' where there were 60 poems.
(F) The name of the sixth collection is 'Kalittokai'. This collection contains 150 love poems. Kapilar was a famous poet of this period.
(G) The name of the seventh collection is 'Akananuru' or 'Netuntokai Paranar' which is a collection of 400 love poems. The famous poets of this period are Pranar and Mamoolanar.
(H) The name of the eighth and last collection is 'Purananuru' where there are 400 poems. Notable among the poets of this collection were Perumaruthanar, Kapilar or Kabilar, Koodalur-Kilar.

The Eighteen Greater Texts: Patinenmelkanakku

Among the eighteen books of ethical poetry, one collection of poems named Naldiar was notable. The name of the second collection of poems was 'Nanmanikkadaikai'. 100 poems written by Nagnar were included in this collection. The next four collections of poems are:

(a) Karnarpathu
(b) Kalbali Narpathu
(c) Itiparbe Nabpathu
(d) Inna Narpathu.

These four collections of poems are also called *Na-Narpathu*. The next four collections of poems are called 'Anthinai'. The poems speak of the happiness that can be found through love marriage and living together. The eleventh book of poetry is the famous book 'Kural' written by Thiruvalluvar. Thiruvalluvar is a well-known name in Tamil literature. In this book of poems, a person's joys and sorrows, happiness and sadness, hopes and aspirations, love and marriage, marital relations are all there. Among the Tamils, the book 'Kural' is equally popular today. Among these poems (a) Eladi, (b) Palmoli, (c) Acharkobai, and (d) Tirikadukam were important. M.V. Arvind commented in the context of the Eighteenth Principle of Poetry or 'Patinenkilkanakku' that the most of the poems in these texts or collections of poems were instructive or principled poems. 'Kural' or 'Tirukkural' is the most significant poem in Sangam literature.

Sangam Literature: Content— Five Epics

Vaidehi Herbert, in his book "Sangam Literature a Beginner's Guide", describe that apart from love and separation, Sangam literature also contains advice, principle and ethics. The reflection of people from all layers of society is there in the Sangam literature. The eternal love of men and women and their separation, hopes and aspirations were the subject of this literature. The grammar book Tolkappiyam was significant in Tamil literature. Although the subject matter of the Tolkappiyam text is grammar, there are also descriptions of what to do when writing a language, the interpretation of different words, people, and their behaviour. There were also various epics in the literary collection. (a) Silappathikaram" or "Silappatikaram,", (b) "Manimekalai", and (c) "Civaka Cintamani" were important. The content of "Silappattikaram" begins with a love story between Kovalan and Madhavi. "Kannaki" was one of the main characters here. 'Manimekalai' was published after "Silappathikaram". Its content is: the story between Kovalan and Manimekalai, daughter of Madhavi. Here Manimekalai became a Buddhist monk and a believer in Buddhist ideology. The theme of "Civaka Cintamani" was: The story of Civaka. She appeared here as a superhuman. The two epics of "Manimekalai" and "Silappathikaram" are called 'Mej Mahakavya'. These two epics were written with the story of the same family. Apart from this, another two epics were (a) Valayapathi and (b) Kundalakeshi. Ilanko Atikal was the author of 'Silappathikaram'. The author of Manimekalai was Kulavanikan Seethabi Satanar. Tiruttakkatevar was the author of "Civaka Cintamani" or Kulavanikan Seethalai Satanar. "Kundalakesi" (Kuntalake-civiruttam) is a Tamil Buddhist epic poem. The author of this book was Nathakuthanaar.

Sangam Era: Society

In his book "*Kanchipuram in Early South Indian History*", T.V. Mahalingam, while describing the social life of the Sangam era, referred to the simple lifestyle of the people of that time. Tamil society was made up of people of different races. The people of the Kirat nation lived in slums. In addition to hunting animals, they were skilled in warfare. They carried arrows, spears, bows and other weapons. The cowherd family was involved in the milk business of cows, sheep and buffaloes. A large section of the population of the Sangam era joined the army. Slaves could be seen in the age of Sangam. The Brahmins were engaged in Yajna and the study of the scriptures. The wives of Brahmins used to cook delicious food for the gods at home. There were no restrictions on eating meat and alcohol. Fishermen used to go to the port and the coast for fishing. The women of the fishermen's house were skilled in dancing. They were called to the royal court. The number of poets was more in the Sangam Era. Most of the poets were poor. Mushiri Puhar, Tonditeban and Mechcha lived in the Tamil region. They were employed as bodyguards or guards in the palace. In the age of Sangam, women have the identity of independent living. They used to participate in various pastimes. The identity of women is also found in the field of education. There were female poets in the Sangam era - Obaira, Bellibidia and others. Many of the women took up dancing and singing as their profession. Men were often interested in having illicit relationships with dancers. The women became proficient in flute, harp playing, painting, flower work and many more. Among the women, lascivious and appealing women used to travel to the royal court. They also served wine to the guests. Various information about marriage was given in the Sangam literature. Arranging meals before the wedding was common. There was a music festival on the occasion of marriage. It is known from the Tolakappiyam and Colbial texts that in the Sangam period it was the guardians who chose the bride of the grooms. In many cases, marriages were performed without their consent. Older women were more likely to marry young men. Dr. Anjali in his book "*Social and Cultural History of Ancient India*" gives an introduction to the worldly life, love and domestic life and family of the Sangam era. The people of the Sangam era had faith in astrology. Men and women wore amulets to fight against evil spirits. It was considered evil for women to keep their hair disheveled. Ceremonies were held for the rain and for protection from the demons.

Sangam Literature: Chera-Pandya-Chola

In the first part of the second volume of "*A Comprehensive History of India*" edited by K.A.N. Shstri, the political life of Tamil Nadu was introduced in the context of Sangam literature. In Sangam literature, three dynasties are known in the case of kings and dynasties. These three dynasties are:

(a) Chera dynasty,
(b) Pandya dynasty, and
(c) Chola dynasty.

Chera Dynasty: Sangam Literature

The Chera dynasty is mentioned in the Sangam literature. The name of Udayanjeral is known among the Chera kings. According to Sangam literature, he entertained the Kauravas and the Pandavas at Kurukshetra and offered them a grand banquet. After Udayanjeral, Chera was ruled by Imayavaramban Nedum Cheral Athan. Nedum Cheralathan is mentioned as the famous Chera king in the poems of the Sangam era. After capturing the Yavanas and bringing them to the capital, he freed them in exchange with a lot of gift items from them. Nedum Cheralathan occupied the territory called Kadambu. In the Sangam poem, Nedunjaral was called the ruler of entire India. He lost his life in the battle with the Cholas. Her two queens practiced Sati by sacrificing their lives on their husband's pyre. His son reigned after Nedum Cheralathan. Chenguttuvanchera (Vel Kezhukuttuvan) was his child. It is known from Sangam literature that he had considerable skills in weaponry, elephant and handling. Apart from the military, he was also culturally famous. The best poet of that time, Parner, was his benefactor. Banji, near Tiruchirappalli, was the capital of the Cheras. The best ruler of another branch of the Cheras was the Shelbakkadungo. Poet Kapilar applauded many of his good deeds such as his generosity and story of winning the war in his peoms. After his death, Tagadur Erinda Perunjeral ascended the throne in Irumporai. Two famous poets: (a) Alathur Kilar and (b) Mosikotnanar were his favourites. Kanikkkal went to Irumporai to clash with the king of Chola, Shengnan. The poet was liberated from Irumporai for a while with the help of his friend Poygair.

Pandya Dynasty: Sangam Literature

Sangam literature has a history of the Pandya dynasty. The story of the Pandya kings was also one of the subjects of Sangam literature. Mudukudumi Perubaludi, a Pandya king, was awarded the title of 'Parameshwar'. The greatest king of the Pandya dynasty was Tayalanganattucheruben Nedungelian. After he ascended the throne a powerful alliance against him invaded the Pandya kingdom. This alliance was made up of 7 kings. These 7 kings are:

(1) Titian
(2) Cher
(3) Chola
(4) Eleni
(5) Porunan
(6) Irungobelman
(6) Erumayuuran.

The enemy thought that this inexperienced Pandya ruler would easily be forced to submit. But the king of Pandya joined the war against the enemy. He entered the Chola kingdom and defeated the enemy. Nedungelian defeated the enemy at the battle of Talaiyalganam. The present name of Talayalanganam is 'Talayalamkandu'. Tolayamkadu was located northwest of the town of *Tirubalur* in Tanjavur district. Nedungelian was well established in the Tamil region with this victory. He gained a reputation as a poet. Nakkirar and Mangudi Kilar wrote praises about Nedungelian. Madurai was the capital of Nedungelian. Ilbandisaipappallittunjiya Nanmaran was a contemporary Pandya king of the poet Nakkiran. He organized Vedic Yajnas. His devotion to God was revealed through worship.

Chola Dynasty: Sangam Literature

In the Sangam literature, the virtues of the Chola kings such as generosity, love of knowledge, rituals of Vedic rituals, Brahmanical devotion, power etc. are found. Poets Parnar and Perungunrup praised the rule of the Chola ruler Ilanjechainni. Karikala was the son of Ilanjechainni. Many poems were written about him in Sangam literature. The god of death, *Yam*, was called Karikala. Karikala won the battle of Belly. Benni, now known as Kobil Benni, situated to the east of the town of Tanjavur. Karikala defeated the combined forces of the Pandya and Cher kings in this battle. The Chola ruler Karikala gained popularity in Tamil Nadu by winning against the Pandyas and Cheras. The poem 'Pattinappalai' written by the poet Urutirangannana contains the story of the conquest of Karikal. This poem mentions that Karikal defeated the Aryans. Karikal reduced the power of the Oliors. In his book "*Kanchipuram in Early South India*", Dr. Venkatanaman Mahalingam of Terlund called the Oliors' as Kalav. The various parts of Tamil Nadu and the southern part of Andhra Pradesh were included in Karikal. Gendaiman Ylandiraiyan was a poet. His poems also found a place in Sangam literature.

11 INDO-GREEK-SAKA-PARTHIAN AND KUSHAN ERA

William Woodthrop Tarn, in his book "*The Greeks: In Bactria and India*", talks about Greek rule and Bactrian rule in ancient India. After the fall of the Mauryan Empire, there were many feeble dynasties in Magadha. During this time, due to political uncertainty, the Bactrian Greeks occupied many areas of the Punjab and the Indus. Later foreign powers like Saka, Pahlava and Kushana dominated various parts of north-west India.

Bactria and Indo-Greek Rule

A.K. Narain recorded many accounts of the Bactrian and Indo-Greek reigns in his book. "*The Indo-Greek: Revisited and Supplemented*". The Balkh region of present-day Afghanistan, or the region bordering the Akshundi River, was known as Bactria. Euthydemus-I intervened when Antiochus, a descendant of Seleucus, tried to recover the Bactria. Antiochus made a treaty with his son Demetrius-I in 206 BC. This incident resulted in the recognition of Bactrian freedom. Antiochus came to India with the help of Bactrian. Antiochus formed an alliance with *Subhagsen* (210 BC), the great-grandson of Asoka, the ruler of Gandhara. Although Antiochus did not come to India, Bactria was the pioneer of the Greek expedition to India. Euthydemus-I dominated southern Afghanistan, establishing Greek rule over bacteria. The descendants of Euthydemus-I conquered southern Afghanistan and the Punjab and the Lower Indus. He introduced coins in Greek and Prakrit. In 171 BC, the general of Demetrius-I, ascended the throne of Bactria. During his tenure a new capital was established at present

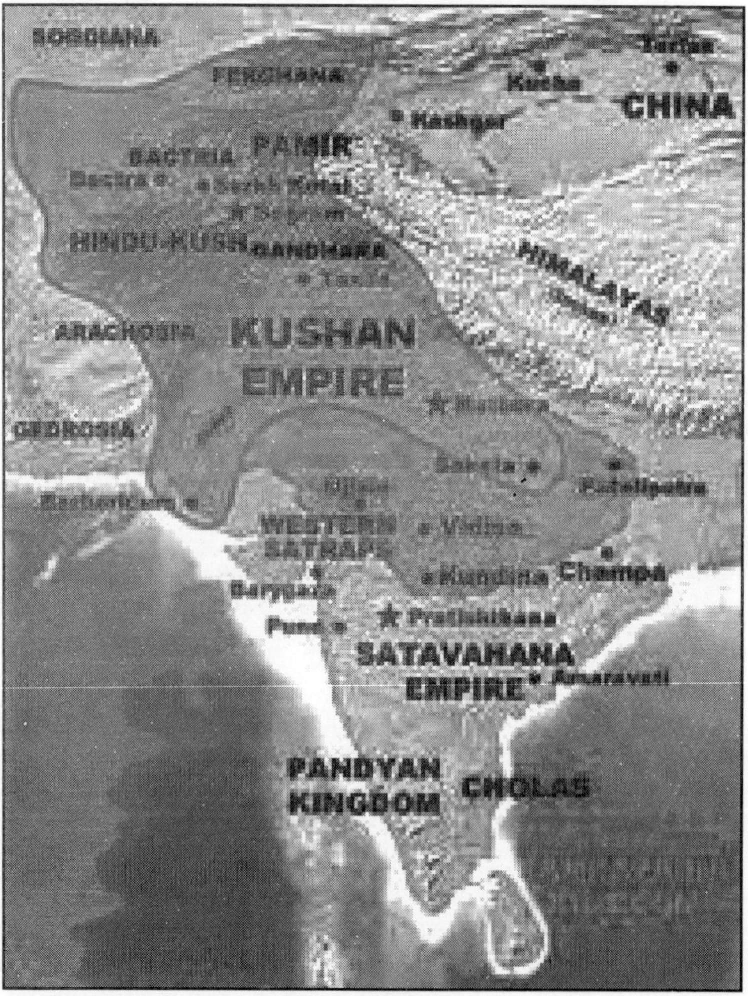

Kushan Empire

Sialkot. After the death of Demetrius in 165 BC, Eucratides-I took over the entire Bactria. After his death the Bactria came into the possession of the Parthians. A section of the Bactrian Greeks ruled in northwestern India. They became known as Indo-Greeks.

Indo-Greek Rule: Menander-I Soter

Esther Edinao and Julia Kindt, in their book, "*The Oxford Handbook of*

Ancient Greek Religion', cite the Indo-Greek ruler Menander-I Soter as being the ruler from 155 BC to 130 BC. Minander ("Menander-I the Saviour", known in Indian Pali sources as Milinda) built a huge empire. His coins were found in the area from Kabul to Mathura. Thomas William Rhys Davids commented in his book '*The Milinda Panha*' that the conversation between the monk Nagasena and Menander-I was the subject of '*Milinda Panho*' written by the Buddhist monk Nagasena. Apart from being a Buddhist, Menander's reputation as a warrior and good ruler was far-reaching. The Bactrian Greeks ruled northwestern India for about 200 years. The Saka, the Parthians, the Pahlava, and the Yu Chi or Kushan invasions put their existence in crisis. The Greek king Hermaens Soter "the Saviour" was defeated by the Pahlava or Parthians and the Bactrian Greek rule came to an end.

Saka Regime

The Sakas were a nomadic people of Central Asia. Horses were their main vehicle. The Greek historian Herodotus mentions in his book that Sakas lived on the shores of the Black Sea. Their original habitat was north of the Syr Darya River in Central Asia. The Sakas advanced southwards, conquering Bactria and Parthia, and advancing towards India through the Kapisa-Gandhara region. The sakas, on the other hand, mingled with the various ethnic groups living in India at that time. During this time their original language changed and they were particularly influenced by Indian culture. However, the Aryans of ancient India did not look at them with much respect. In Patanjali's commentary, they have been called 'pure Shudras'. On the other hand, in the "*Manu Samhita*" they are called 'lower Kshatriyas'. In ancient India, they were known as 'Kshatrap' to the common people. Judging by the location, they had two branches. These two branches were named - Northern Kshatrap and Western Kshatrap. The northern Kshatrap was called the Kshatrap of Takshashila and Mathura region and the western Kshatrap was called the Kshatrap of Saurashtra region. The first Saka king to be mentioned in India was Manes or Moga. It is known from the Takshashila discipline and copper coins that he was probably the ruler of Gandhara. He ruled over Gandhara and West Punjab in about 80 BC. The next king of

Moga was Aages. He defeated the descendants of the Bactrian king Euthydemus-I and brought East Punjab under his control. Apart from northern India, the Sakas also extended their empire to the west and south. The capital of this part was Nashik. Their territory was Malava (Malwa), Kathiawar and parts of Maharashtra. The saka rulers took the titles 'Kshatrap (Kshaharata)' and 'Mahakshatrap'. It is known from various inscriptions and coins that there were two Kshatrapas named Bhumika and Nahapana. Nahapana is the best of these two. He was able to capture a large part of Maharashtra from the kings of the Satavahana dynasty. Nahpana was king from 119 to 124 AD. His empire extended to (a) North Konkan, (b) Ajmer, (c) Maharashtra, and (d) Kathiawar. But later Gautamiputra Satakarni of the Satavahana dynasty was able to restore the kingdom by defeating Nahapana. Ujjain was the main centre of the Sakas in western India. Another branch of the Sakas was called Kardamaka (Bhadramukhas). "Satrap" *Chashtana* was the founder of this dynasty. Dr. Jitendranath Banerjee in his book "*A Comprehensive History of India*" mentions *Chashtana* as the founder of the 'Kardamaka (Chastana)' branch. The group was named Kardamaka after the Kardam River in the Bactrian region of Persia. Sylvan refers to Levy *Chashtana* as "the son of Yashmotik." *Chashtana* rescued some parts of the kingdom from the Satavahanas. Later, King Rudradamana-I of this dynasty defeated Satakarni in 130 AD. According to Ptolemy's writings and Junagadh inscriptions, *Rudradaman-I* defeated the Satavahanas and recaptured Malwa. In this situation, Gautamiputra Satakarni married his own son to the daughter of *Rudradaman-I* for the purpose of establishing friendly relations with the Sakas. The orthodox Brahmin Gautamiputra Satakarni was forced to establish relations with *Rudradaman-I* and Indianize the Saka race. So this marriage had social significance in addition to its political significance. The list of areas under *Rudradaman-I* is available from the Junagadh inscription:

(a) Akravanti or East Malava and Avanti or West Malwa,
(b) Mahishmati,
(c) East of Junagadh,
(d) North Kathiawar,
(e) North Konkan,

(f) Adjacent to Dwarka,
(g) Coastal area of Savarmati river,
(h) Kachchha,
(i) West Vindhyachal,
(j) Indus Valley area.

It is further known from this inscription that *Rudradaman-I* built a beautiful lake near Girnar for the benefit of the people. *Rudradaman-I* was a scholar and a fan of Sanskrit literature. The Saka rule in western India was ended by the Gupta emperor Chandragupta-II.

Pahlava Rule or Parthian Rule

The Pahlavas were originally of Iranian descent. The dynasty was founded around 273 BC. They come to India from Iran. However, unlike other dynasties, the Pahlavas are not considered as important in the political history of India. They were able to establish a kingdom in Takshashila in the middle of the first century AD. That was the extent of their kingdom. Dr. Hemchandra Roychowdhury commented in his book "*The Political History of India*" that the 'Pahlava' people lived on the south-eastern shores of the Caspian Sea. Pahlava belonged to the sixteenth province of the Persian Empire of the Persian Emperor Darius. They were known as Parthians because they lived in Parthia. The Parthians became independent under the leadership of a Parthian hero named *Argsen*. In India, the Parthians were known as 'Pahlava'. Between 171-131 BC, Pahlava tried to enter India by conquering the Bactrian Mithridetis. The Pahlavas took over part of Gandhara from the Sakas. Gondophernes was the most important of the Pahlava kings in the north-western part of India. Parts of the kingdom of Gondophernes were southern Afghanistan, Peshawar, East Gandhara, Lower Indus region, etc. The inscription "Takht-i-Bahi" found in Peshawar states that Gondophernes was the provincial ruler of *Arachosia*. According to the inscription 'Takht-i-Bahi', he is believed to have ruled from 21-46. He ended the Bactrian rule by defeating Hameus, the Bactrian ruler of Kabul. Gondophernes converted to Christianity at the initiative of St. Thomas, a Christian priest. After the death of Gondophernes his kingdom or Pahlava kingdom was weakened. The Kushan rulers then destroyed the Pahlava dominance in the Indus and Punjab regions.

Kushan Era

Dr. K.N. Banerjee and Professor Jagannath, in their book "*A Comprehensive History of India*", discussed about the Yuezhi (Yueh-chih) group while discussing the origin of the Kushans. The Yuezhi group was mentioned in the book "The book of the Later Han". "The Book of the Later Han", also known as the "History of the Later Han" and by its Chinese name "Hou Hanshu". Of these, the Guishung group was known as the Kushans in India. Miyats is known as the first ruler of the Kushans. The Kushans were a branch of the Yuethi nation. According to "Hou Hanshu", Kujula Kadphises became the leader of the Kushans.

Kushan Period: Kujula Kadphises (c. 30-c. 80)

The reign of Kujula Kadphises was 15-65 years. He assumed the title of King or Wang by uniting the 'Yuezhi' group or their branches. He captured Kabul and Kashmir from the Pahlavas. The dominance of Kujula Kadphises in Bactria was also established. After the conquest of Gandhara, Kujula Kadphises took his title. His empire expanded from the Persian border to the Indus region. He introduced coins in his own name. He converted to Buddhism.

Vima Taktu or Vima Takto (c. 80 - c. 95)

Vima Takto or Vima Taktu was a Kushan emperor who reigned C. 90-113 C.E. Vima Takto was long known as "The nameless king", since his coins only showed the legend "The King of Kings", "Great Saviour", until discovery of the Rabatak inscription helped connect his name with the title on the coins. Vima Takto's empire covered northesterm Gandhara and greater Bactria towards China, where Kushan presence has been asserted in the Tarim Basin. Under his reign, embassies were also sent to the Chinese court. He expanded the Kushan Empire into the northwest of South-Asia. He was the predecessor of Vima Kadphises, and Kanishka-I.

Vima Kadphises (c. 95-c. 127)

After the death of Kujula Kadphises, his son Vima Kadphises or the second Kadphises ascended the throne. He was known as 'Yen-Cao Chen'. He ascended the Kushan throne as Kadphises-II and his empire spread to present-day Uttar Pradesh. He took the titles of 'Sarvalokeshwar', 'Mahishwar', 'Maharaj', 'Rajadhiraja'. Gold coins are believed to have been first introduced in India during his reign. During his reign, India's trade with China and the Roman Empire increased.

Kanishka-I (78 - Approximately 102 A.D.)

Kanishka-I or Kanishka the Great was a Kushan emperor. He is famous in the history of India for his military, political and spiritual activities. *Kanishka-I* was the successor of Kujula Kadphises, the founder of the Kushan Empire. Dr. Hemchandra Roychowdhury in his book "*Political History of Ancient India*" discusses the achievements of *Kanishka's* conquest of the kingdom as well as the context of his religious patronage.

Kanishka's Accession to the Throne: Debate

There is disagreement among scholars as to exactly when *Kanishka-I* ascended the throne. According to Rapson, Ferguson and Oldenberg, *Kanishka-I* ascended the throne in the year 78 AD. Dr. Hemchandra Roychowdhury and the historian Thomas have spoken in support of this view. Dr. Bratindranath Mukherjee in his book "Rise and Fall of the Kushana Empire" states that 'Shakabda' was started during the Kushan period in that year, i.e. 78 AD. *Kanishka-I* was the initiator of this 'Shakabda'. It is implemented and used by the Sakas. They accepted the dominance of the Kushans. Shakabda was started in recognition of the acceptance of Kushan domination. *Kanishka-I* introduced Shakabda to mark the period of his accession to the throne. However, it should be noted that *Kanishka-I* himself was not a Saka. Adding 78-79 years to AD, one would get the Shakabda.

Kanishka-I: Expansion of the Empire

Among the foreign nations that came to India after the fall of the Mauryan Empire and expanded their empire, the Kushans are notable among them. Kanishka-I (C. 127-C. 150) was the best king of this Kushan dynasty. Determining the exact boundaries of his conquests and empires is not at all easy. According to the historian Ranbir Chakravarti, the expansion of Kanishka's empire can be traced back to Chinese, Tibetan and Indian elements. *Kanishka-I* conquered Magadha. From Magadha, the Buddhist philosopher Asvaghosa went to the Kushan capital, Purushapur. According to Hiuen Tsang, the capital of Kanishka's vast empire was Purushapura or present-day Peshawar. According to the Rabatak inscription, Kanishka's royal order is listed in all the regions where it was observed. (a) Sanketa, (b) Ujjain, (c) Pataliputra, (d) Kaushambi, (e) Srichampa, etc. regions belonged to the *Kanishka-I* Empire. *Kanishka-I* also tried to expand his empire outside India. Peshawar, Rawalpindi, Kashmir, Mathura, Sravasti were under the Kushan Empire. Various regions of Central Asia belonged to the Kushan Empire, the most notable of which were:

(a) Kashgar,
(b) Khotan, and
(c) Yarkand.

Apart from Purushapura or Peshawar, the capital of *Kanishka-I*, the Balkh region of Bactria was the heart of the Kushan Empire. According to Hiuen Tsang's book 'Si-Yu-Ki', the eastern part of the Pamir region belonged to the *Kanishka-I* Empire. The *Kanishka-I* Empire stretched from the border of the Gobi Desert in the north-west to Magadha and Varanasi in the east.

Kanishka-I: Evaluation

The contribution of *Kanishka-I*, the best emperor of the Kushans, is multifaceted. During his time there was an unprecedented improvement in industrial architecture. Notable examples of this architecture is Gandhara art. According to Dr. Ramesh Chandra Majumdar, the hands of Gandhara's art were both Greek, but the heart was Indian. Stupas, monasteries and chaityas were built under the patronage of *Kanishka-I*. For *Kanishka-I*, Buddhism spread to many parts of the world. He himself converted to Buddhism and built a chaitya in Peshawar. This monastery was one of the centres of Buddhist worship. It was during Kanishka's time that the fourth Buddhist music took place in Jalandhar. Basumitra IV was the president of Buddhist music. *Asvaghosa* became the vice-president. *Kanishka-I* converted to Mahayana Buddhism and propagated it elsewhere in the world. *Kanishka-I* was instrumental in the propagation of Buddhism outside India. Through his efforts, Buddhism spread to Khotan, China, Japan and Korea. According to Vincent Smith, *Kanishka-I* was the second Asoka in the history of Buddhism. Apart from Buddhism, *Kanishka-I* was also sympathetic to Jainism. *Kanishka-I* also deserves considerable credit as a patron of literature and culture. *Asvaghosa*, the author of "*Buddhacharita*", Nagarjuna, a Buddhist philosopher, a proponent of secondary and nihilistic philosophy, Basumitra, a Buddhist writer, Charaka, a renowned physician, author of the book "*Charak Sanhita*", Agesilas, an architect, Mathar, a politician, etc. were the notable people during the reign of *Kanishka-I*. Asvaghosa was the best writer during his time. Apart from "*Buddhacharita*", the other three books written by *Asvaghosa* are:

(a) *Sariputta Prakaran*,
(b) *Sutralankara*, and
(c) *Saundarananda*.

Kanishka-I was instrumental in building numerous Buddhist monasteries, stupas and chaityas. During his time four different art forms appeared in Sarnath, Mathura, Gandhara and Amravati. *Kanishka-I* used to call himself 'Devputra'. Notable among his ministers and advisers were *Asvaghosa* and *Charaka*. The progress of Indo-Roman trade was also noticed during the *Kanishka-I* period. Dr. Bratindranath Mukherjee thinks that significant progress was made in the economy of India during the *Kanishka-I* period.

BIBLIOGRAPHY

Agrawal, D.P., *The Archaeology of India*, 1985.

Basham, A.L., *The Wonder that was India*, 1971.

Basham, A.L., ed., *A Cultural History of India*, 1975.

Briget and F. Raymond Allchin, *The Rise of Civilization in India and Pakistan*, 1983.

Chakarabarti, D.K., *An Oxford Companion to India Archaeology*, 2006.

Chakrabarti, Dilip Kumar, *India: Archaeological History*, 1997.

Chakravarti, Uma, *The Social Dimensions of Early Buddhism*, 1997.

Champakalaskshmi, R., *Trade, Ideology and Urbanization: South India 300 BC-AD 1300*, 1996.

Gunukkal, Rajan, *Social Formations of Early South India*, 2010.

Habib, Irfan, *A People's History, Vol. 1: Pre-History*, 2001.

Habib, Irfan, *A People's History, Vol. 2: Indus Civilization: Including Other Copper Age Cultures and the History of Language Change till 155 BC*, 2002.

Jha, D.N., *Ancient India in Historical Outline*, 1998.

Jha, D.N., *Ancient India: An Introduction*, 1998.

Kosambi, D.D., *An Introduction to the Study of Indian History*, 1956.

Raychaudhuri, H.C., *Political History of Ancient India*, Rev. ed. with Commentary by B.N. Mukherjee, 1996.

Sastri, K.A.N., ed., *History of South India*, 1966.

Sharma, R.S., *India's Ancient Past*, 2007.

Sharma, R.S., *Looking for the Aryans*, 1995.

Sharma, R.S., *Material Culture and Social Formations in Ancient India*, 1983.

Singh, Upinder, *A History of Ancient and Early Medieval India*, 2008.

Thapar, Romila, *Ashoka and the Decline of the Mauryas*, 1997.

Thapar, Romila, *Early India from Beginnings to 1300*, 2002.

NOTES

NOTES

NOTES

NOTES